Morris E. Ruddick is president of Ruddick Research International, Inc., a full-service market and communication research firm with offices in Tulsa, Houston, New York, and San Francisco. He is involved in research in corporate image, media, consumer marketing, employee attitude, and public-opinion–related studies. He was formerly a project director for an industrial market research consulting operation. He holds a master's degree from Oklahoma State University in research design and analysis and has completed additional graduate courses in multivariate statistical analysis.

Philip K. Sherwood is executive vice president of Ruddick Research International, Inc. His background includes research projects in marketing and financial planning, and he has taught undergraduate and graduate courses in Oral Roberts University's graduate School of Business. He holds a B.A., an M.B.A., and a doctorate in administration from Indiana University.

Robert E. Stevens is a professor of marketing in ORU's graduate School of Business. He has done research and consulting work for a variety of firms at both the local and national level, and he has taught marketing research at the graduate level since 1969. He holds an M.B.A. and a Ph.D. in marketing from the University of Arkansas, and he has written several books and articles.

THE MARKETING RESEARCH HANDBOOK

A DECISION-ORIENTED APPROACH

Morris E. Ruddick
Philip K. Sherwood
Robert E. Stevens

A SPECTRUM BOOK

Prentice-Hall, Inc., Englewood Cliffs, New Jersey 07632

Library of Congress Cataloging in Publication Data

Ruddick, Morris E.
　　The marketing research handbook.

　　"A Spectrum Book."
　　Includes index.
　　1. Marketing research.　　I. Sherwood, Philip K.
II. Stevens, Robert E. (date).　　III. Title.
HF5415.2.R82　1983　　　658.8'3　　　83-3093
ISBN 0-13-557736-5
ISBN 0-13-557728-4 (pbk.)

10　9　8　7　6　5　4　3　2　1

ISBN 0-13-557736-5

ISBN 0-13-557728-4 {PBK.}

Editorial/production supervision by Peter Jordan
Cover design © 1983 by Jeannette Jacobs
Manufacturing buyer: Cathie Lenard

Prentice-Hall International, Inc., *London*
Prentice-Hall of Australia Pty. Limited, *Sydney*
Prentice-Hall Canada Inc., *Toronto*
Prentice-Hall of India Private Limited, *New Delhi*
Prentice-Hall of Japan, Inc., *Tokyo*
Prentice-Hall of Southeast Asia Pte. Ltd., *Singapore*
Whitehall Books Limited, *Wellington, New Zealand*
Editora Prentice-Hall do Brasil Ltda., *Rio de Janeiro*

This book is dedicated to God, who makes all things possible, and to our wives—Carol Ruddick, Jean Sherwood, and Liz Stevens—who supported our efforts unselfishly.

Contents

Preface

This book is designed primarily for two groups of readers. The first group consists of managers who must negotiate, evaluate, and use marketing research as a part of the decision-making process. The second group includes those individuals involved in the research process who need to review marketing research procedures or find examples of specific techniques. This book could also serve as the basic text for an introductory course in marketing research, especially if the course takes a research project approach.

Three primary considerations were used in preparing the book. The first was length. We wanted to keep the amount of reading material brief enough to be read and reviewed quickly. Therefore, we had to omit many topics and provide only a limited discussion of others. However, the essential concepts and techniques are presented in a much more concise form.

The second consideration was to present material that was theoretically sound but practically oriented. We wanted the reader to be able to put the concepts presented to immediate use in decision making. A unique feature of this book is that it describes the major forecasting, sampling, and analysis techniques without using mathematical formulas.

The final consideration was to provide a thorough set of appendices to illustrate various aspects of a research project, such as a research proposal, questionnaire, or final report. Thus, the reader can not only read about a research proposal but can actually see what one looks like.

This is useful in preparing proposals or in evaluating proposals done by others. A glossary of marketing research terms is included as a ready reference to commonly used marketing research terminology.

The result, we believe, is a book that is both readable and helpful to those involved with research. We hope this book serves you as a tutorial and as an easily accessible reference for research projects.

Acknowledgments

A book is seldom the work of the authors alone but constitutes the input of many people. Some of the people we would like to specifically acknowledge are: Dewey Hicks, of Ruddick Research Inc., for compiling the statistical tables in the appendix; Marcella Rodgers, for supervising and/or typing the many drafts of this book; Jane Olsen, who helped prepare the authors' information and put finishing touches on the typing; Carl Hamilton, provost of Oral Roberts University, for providing the support for typing and duplicating the manuscript; and, finally, John Hunger, acquisitions editor, General Publishing Division, and the editing and production staff at Prentice-Hall, Inc., for their expertise in putting together a book such as this. To all these people we are truly grateful.

Any errors of omission or commission, however, remain the sole responsibility of the authors.

chapter one

Introduction to
Marketing Research

THE MARKETING
DECISION ENVIRONMENT

letter

Marketing decisions in contemporary organizations are some of the most important decisions made by managers. The decisions about which consumer segments to serve with what products or services, at what prices, through which channels, and with what type and amounts of promotion not only determine the marketing posture of a firm but also affect decisions in other areas. The decision to emphasize quality products, for example, places restraints on procurement, production personnel, quality control, and so on.

Many companies are discovering that the decisions involved in creating and distributing goods and services to selected consumer segments have such long-range implications for the organization that they are now being viewed as strategic decisions requiring input by top management. Some marketing decisions, such as those relating to strategy, may involve commitments and directions that are never departed from if they are initially successful.

The importance of these strategic decisions and the operating decisions made to implement them has increased the importance of the intelligence function within organizations. Marketing research is the specific marketing function relied on to provide information on which to base marketing decisions.

MARKETING RESEARCH

Research in a business context is defined as an organized, formal inquiry into an area to obtain information for use in decision making. When the adjective *marketing* is added to *research,* the context of the area of inquiry is defined. Marketing research, then, refers to procedures and techniques involved in the design, data collection, analysis, and presentation of information used in making marketing decisions. More succinctly, *marketing research produces the information managers need to make marketing decisions.*

Although many of the procedures used to conduct marketing research can also be used in other types of research, marketing decisions require approaches that fit the decision-making environment to which they are being applied. Marketing research can make its greatest contribution to management when the researcher understands the environment, industry, management goals and styles, and decision processes that give rise to the need for information.

MARKETING RESEARCH
AND DECISION MAKING

Although the performance of the activities that constitute marketing research requires a variety of research techniques, the focus of marketing research should not be on research techniques. The focus should be on the decisions to be made and not the techniques used to collect the information used to make the decisions. Nothing is more central to understanding the marketing research function and to effectively and efficiently using research in decision making. Any user or provider of marketing research who loses sight of this central focus is likely to end up in one of two awkward and costly positions: (1) failing to collect the information actually needed to make a decision, or (2) collecting information that is not needed in a given decision-making context. The result of the first situation is ineffectiveness—not reaching a desired objective. The result of the second is inefficiency—failing to reach an objective in the least costly manner. The chances of either of these problems occurring are greatly reduced when the decision itself is the focus of the research effort.

To maintain this focal point, one must understand the purpose and role of marketing research in decision making. *The basic purpose of marketing research is to reduce uncertainty or error in decision making.* The uncertainty of the outcomes surrounding a decision is what makes decision making difficult. If you knew for sure the outcome of choosing one alternative over another, then choosing the right alternative would

2

be simple, given the decision-making criteria. If you know for sure that alternative A would result in $100,000 in profit and alternative B would result in $50,000 in profit, and if the decision criterion was to maximize profits, then the choice of alternative A would be obvious. However, business decisions must be made under conditions of uncertainty—you can't know for sure if alternative A will produce $50,000 more than B. In fact, either or both alternatives may result in losses. The degree of uncertainty surrounding a decision, the importance of the decision, and the amount of uncertainty that the information will reduce cause information to have value.

Decision making is defined as *a choice among alternative courses of action*. This four-step process involves (1) identifying a problem or opportunity, (2) defining the problem or opportunity, (3) identifying alternative courses of action, and (4) selecting a specific course of action.

STEPS IN DECISION MAKING			
Step 1	*Step 2*	*Step 3*	*Step 4*
Recognize the Existence of Problems and Opportunities	Define the Exact Nature of Problems and Opportunities	Identify Alternative Courses of Action	Select an Alternative Course of Action

Recognizing the Existence of Problems and Opportunities

A problem or opportunity is the focus of management efforts to maintain or restore performance. A problem is anything that stands in the way of achieving an objective. An opportunity is a chance to improve an overall performance.

Managers need information to help them recognize problems and opportunities. A problem must be recognized before it can be defined and alternatives developed. An example of this type of information is attitudinal data that compare attitudes toward competing brands. Attitudes are usually predictive of sales behavior. Therefore, if attitudes toward a company's product become less favorable than before, the attitudinal information can make the managers aware of the existence of a problem.

Defining the Problem or Opportunity

Once a problem or opportunity has been recognized, it must be defined. Until a clear definition of the problem is established, no alternative courses of action can be considered. The symptoms of the problem are recognized first, and there may be several problems that produce the same set of symptoms. This is analogous to someone with a headache (symptom), who may be suffering from a sinus infection, stress, the flu, or a host of other illnesses (potential problems). Treating the headache may provide temporary relief, but not dealing with the root problem will ensure its return, perhaps worsening physical conditions.

The same type of phenomenon occurs in marketing. A decline in sales (symptom) may be the result of a decline in total industry sales, lower prices by competitors, low product quality, or a myriad of other potential problems. No alternative courses of action should be considered until the actual problem is defined. Information aids the manager at this stage in the decision-making process by defining the problem.

In some cases an entire research project must be devoted to defining the problem or identifying an opportunity formerly overlooked because of a lack of insight or prior knowledge of a particular area. This type of study is usually called an *exploratory study* and is discussed more fully in chapter three.

Identifying Alternatives

The third stage in the decision-making process involves identifying viable alternatives. For some problems, developing alternatives is a natural outcome of defining the problem, especially if that particular problem or opportunity has occurred before. A manager's past knowledge and experiences are used to develop the alternatives in these situations. However, in other situations a real contribution of research is to inform the decision maker of the options available to him. A company considering introduction of a new product may use consumer information to evaluate different ways in which their new product might be positioned in the market. Information about the significant product attributes and how these products are positioned in the consumer's mind would be an evaluation of possible "openings" (options) available.

Selecting an Alternative

The final stage in the decision-making process is the choice among the alternative courses of action available to the decision maker. Information provided by research can aid a manager at this stage by estimating the effects of the various alternatives on the decision criteria. For example, a firm considering introduction of a new product might develop and test market two versions of that product. The two versions are two alternatives to be considered, and the sales and profits resulting from the test marketing provide the information needed to choose one alternative. Another example is the pretest of television commercials using different themes, characters, and scripts to obtain information on consumer reactions to the different commercials. This information helps to determine the best advertising approaches to use.

Information collected through research must be directly related to the decision in order to accomplish the purpose of risk reduction. Thus, the focus of research should be on the decision-making processes in general and, specifically, the decision to be made in a given situation rather than the data or the techniques used to collect the data. There is always the danger that a person involved in marketing research might view himself or herself as a research technician rather than as someone who provides information to help managers make decisions. Thus, the information produced through a research project must be determined by the decision to be made by a manager.

STRATEGIC VS. TACTICAL INFORMATION NEEDS

Managers are called upon to make two basic types of decisions—strategic and tactical. The strategic decisions are those that have long-range implications and effects. These decisions are critical to a firm's success and may not be altered if they are successful. Tactical decisions are short-term in scope and effect and are usually altered on a regular basis. Examples of these two types of decisions will help clarify the distinction, which many researchers and managers have failed to understand.

A company analyzing an industry for possible entry would be considering a strategic move—entering a new industry. This requires information about such things as competitor strengths and weaknesses; market shares held by competitors; market growth potential; production, financial, and marketing requirements for success in the industry; and strategic tendencies of competitors. This is *strategic* information. Once the decision to enter the industry has been made, then information about current prices charged by specific competitors, current package designs and sizes, and so on, is needed to make the tactical decisions for the short run—a year or less. This is *tactical* information.

Strategic decisions require strategic information, and tactical decisions require tactical information. Failure to recognize this distinction between decision types and information types will result in information for the right areas, such as prices, but with the wrong time frame. For tactical decisions, a manager needs to know competitive prices and their importance to both competitors and consumers. For strategic decisions, the manager is more interested in competitors' abilities and tendencies to use pricing as a retaliatory weapon.

The researcher and the manager must be sure that the time frame for the decision is specified in advance to ensure that the right type of information is collected. This should be a joint effort by both the user and the provider of the information.

Steps in a Research Project
— 1. Define the Management Problem
— 2. State Research Objectives
— 3. Develop Research Methodology
—   a. Define information problem—specific information needs
—   b. Define population to be studied
—   c. Develop sampling technique and determine sample size
—   d. Determine how to measure variables or attributes to be studied
     e. Determine how to collect data
     f. Determine how to analyze data
— 4. Collect Data
— 5. Analyze and Interpret Data
— 6. Present Findings
     a. Technical report
     b. Popular report

STEPS IN A MARKETING RESEARCH PROJECT

Ensuring that data collected in a research project not only is related to management's information needs but also fits management's time frame requires a research approach that is centered on the management problem—the decision to be made. This approach is divided into two phases—the planning phase and the execution phase.

An old work adage states, "Plan your work, work your plan," and this approach should be used in carrying out a research project. A research project does not begin with a questionnaire, a focus-group interview, or any other research technique, but with a carefully thought-out plan for the research, including: (1) a statement of the management problem or opportunity, (2) a set of research objectives, and (3) a statement of the research methodology to be used in the project.

The Management Problem

The starting point in a research project should be an attempt by both the user and the provider of information to clearly define the problem. Nowhere in the research process is their mutual understanding and agreement more necessary than at this point. Failure by either party to understand or clearly define the major issue will surely lead to disappointment and wasted effort. Many information users, especially the uninitiated, have been "burnt," never to be "burnt" again, by someone who has collected some data, collected their money, and left them with a lot of "useful" information. A health care administrator recently related such a story. He had heard a lot about marketing and the need to have information about consumers, although he was really unclear about both. He was approached by a marketing research firm who offered to supply a lot of "useful marketing information" for a reasonable fee. Several months after he had received the final report and the marketing research firm had received his check, he realized that he had no idea how to use the information or if it was what he really needed.

This type of problem can be avoided, or at least minimized, through user-provider interaction, analysis, and discussion of the key management issues involved in the situation. The information provider's task is to convert the manager's statement of symptoms into a list of likely problems and decision issues and then, finally, information issues. Two key questions must always be asked at this stage: (1) What information does the decision maker feel is needed to make a specific decision? and (2) How will the information be used to make the decision? Asking these questions will cause the information user to begin thinking about the information needed rather than the decision itself. Also, the user can start thinking specifically about how the information will be used.

An example of this interaction process will help clarify this point. An executive vice-president for a franchise of a national motel-restaurant chain was evaluating his information needs with one of the authors about a major remodeling of one of the chain's restaurants. The author posed the question about how the information was going to be used in the decision-making process. The vice-president then realized that corporate policy would not permit deviation from the established interior designs currently used even if information were available indicating that a different design would be more acceptable to consumers. He then concluded that he didn't need the information! The information could have been obtained easily through a survey, but management would have been unable to act on it. The manager realized that he needed to work on a policy change at the corporate level and that any information that would be needed would be used to evaluate that particular policy.

Clearly defining the real management issues must be foremost in the researcher's thinking. Information, regardless of quality or quantity, collected for the wrong problem or unrelated to the right decision represents wasted resources and may even mislead management. The relationship of information needs to strategy decisions in marketing will be further discussed in chapter 2.

If the problem cannot be defined based on current information, an entire study may be necessary. As was mentioned earlier, this is a project in itself and is called *exploratory research*. The problem in the exploratory study is to identify the variables in a given management situation and to develop a clear definition of the problem or opportunity facing the organization.

Research Objectives

There is a logical flow from the statement of the problem to the identification of specific objectives to be accomplished in the research project. The objectives represent a decomposition of the problem into a series of statements that constitute the end results sought through the research project. The objectives should be stated so that their accomplishment will provide the information necessary to solve the problem. The objectives serve to guide the research results by providing the direction and scope of a given project, and they are the basis for developing the project's methodology.

Objectives are another area in which the user and provider should interact so that the research will produce results that both the user and provider are anticipating. The information provider's role is usually to interpret needs and develop a list of objectives that serve as a basis of negotiation for final research objectives.

Research Methodology

After the management problem has been defined and research objectives agreed upon by both user and provider, the next step in the research process is to develop a research methodology that will accomplish the objectives and provide the information needed to solve the management problem. Overall research designs will be dealt with at length in chapter 3. The purpose here is to explain and identify the decisions that must be made in developing the methodology.

Defining Information Needs. The first step in developing the research methodology is to identify the specific types of information needed to accomplish the research objectives. While this might appear to be an inherent part of the process of developing the objectives, it is usually wise to approach this in a more formal way by identifying specific information types. For example, let's say a research objective was stated as follows: Identify the characteristics of heavy users, light users, and nonusers of the product. The word "characteristics" can take on a wide variety of definitions—socioeconomic, psychological, behavioral, and physical. What specific types of information are needed in this particular research project? Answering this question forces the researcher to evaluate information sought with objectives and the management problem in mind.

This step could be completed under the measurement area—deciding what is to be measured—and this is acceptable. However, since every aspect of research methodology is directly influenced by the type of information to be collected and analyzed, there are advantages to using this as the initial step in methodology.

Population or Universe. The next step in developing the research methodology is to define the population or universe of the study. The research *universe* includes all of the people, stores, or places that possess some characteristic that management is interested in measuring. The universe must be defined for each research project, and this defined universe becomes the group from which a sample is drawn. The list of all universe elements is sometimes referred to as the *sampling frame*.

It is extremely important that the sampling frame include *all* members of the population. Failure to meet this requirement can result in bias. If, for example, you were trying to estimate the average income in a given area and were going to use the telephone book as your sampling frame, three problems would be encountered. First, not everyone has a telephone and those who do not tend to be in a low-income bracket. Second, 15 to 20 percent of phone owners have unlisted numbers. Third, new residents would not be listed. The difference between the sampling frame (telephone book) and area residents could be substantial and could bias the results.

It is imperative that the population be carefully identified by using a sampling technique that minimizes the chance of bias. Techniques for successfully avoiding such biases will be discussed in chapter 7.

Sampling Technique and Sample Size. Two separate decisions are called for in this step. The first is to determine how specific sample elements will be drawn from the population. There are two broad categories of sampling techniques: probability and nonprobability. The approach selected depends on the nature of the problem and the nature of the population under study. For probability sample designs, the objective is to draw a sample that is both representative and useful. For nonprobability designs, the objective is to select a useful sample even though it may not be representative of the population. These distinctions will be clarified later, but it is important to note that the sample design influences the applicability of various types of statistical analysis; some analysis types are directly dependent upon how sample elements are drawn.

Sample size represents the other side of the decision. Determining how many sample elements are needed to accomplish the research objectives requires both analysis and judgment. The techniques for determining sample size are discussed in chapter 7, along with a whole series of other nonstatistical questions such as costs, response rate, and homogeneity of sample elements, which must be considered when deciding on sample size. In some studies the cost may dictate a lower sample size than would be required for sampling reliability.

Measurement Decisions. Another tough question is "How will we measure what we need to measure?" The answer is one of the most difficult ones facing the researcher. If attitudes are to be measured, for example, techniques to be chosen from include the method of equal appearing intervals, the semantic differential, and the Likert technique. In many cases no validating measuring techniques are available, so the researcher must rely on what has been used in past studies and on his or her own judgment to decide upon the appropriate technique.

It is extremely important for the researcher to develop operational definitions of the concepts to be measured, and these definitions must be stated explicitly. Even seemingly simple concepts, such as awareness, can be defined in several ways, with each definition having different meaning and relative importance. For 60 percent of the respondents to say they had heard of Kleenex is not the same as 60 percent saying that Kleenex is what comes to mind when they think of facial tissues. Yet both of these approaches measure awareness.

Once the planning stages are complete, the written results of the plan should be embodied in a document called a *research proposal*. A proposal should be prepared whether the project is done in-house or by an outside research organization because it is the basis for allocating funds internally and for a contract agreement when an outside firm is involved. If an outside firm is used, their staff normally prepares the proposal based on interaction with the information users and those with authority to expend funds for outside research. (Two sample research proposals are presented in appendix A.)

Data Collection. The next decision area is how to collect the data. The first choice is between observation and interrogation, and the second choice is which specific observation or interrogation technique to use. These decisions, in turn, depend on what information is needed, from which sample elements, in what time frame, and at what level of cost.

Data collection can be the single most costly element in a project or it can be of low relative cost, depending on the nature of the project. However, data collection is always an important determinant of research value because of the influence of the conditions surrounding data collection on the validity of the results obtained.

Using untrained interviewers to collect data, for example, can produce not only invalid data, but also data that can mislead management into making a wrong decision. Careful control of data collection is essential to effective research. Data collection problems and techniques are examined in detail in chapters 4–6.

Data Analysis. One final research methodology decision area concerns the methods used to analyze the data. The major criterion here is the nature of the data to be analyzed. The purpose of the analysis is to obtain meaning from the raw data that have been collected.

For many researchers the area of data analysis can be the most troublesome. Choosing the appropriate technique and carrying out the calculations, or reading them from a computer printout, is the difference between the seasoned researcher and the novice in many situations. Failure to use the appropriate techniques can result in not getting enough out of the available data or trying to go beyond the data limits in the analysis. The basis for good data analysis techniques is discussed in chapter 8.

Collecting, Analyzing, Interpreting, and Presenting Results

Once the above steps have been completed and the planning stage of the research project has been carried out, you are now ready for the execution stages. The execution stages involve carrying out the research plan, collecting the data from the population sampled in the ways specified, and analyzing the data using the techniques already identified in the research plan. If the research plan or proposal has been well thought out and "debugged" through revisions of objectives and research designs, then the implementation steps will flow much better and may be completed in a few weeks.

Once the data are collected and analyzed, the researcher must interpret the results of the findings in terms of the management problem. This means determining what the results imply about the solution to the management problems and recommending a course of action to management. If the purpose of the research project was to determine the feasibility of introducing a new product and the results of the research project show that the product will produce an acceptable level of profits, then the researcher should recommend introduction of the product unless there are known internal or external barriers that cannot be overcome. This means that the researcher must move beyond the role of the scientist in objectively collecting and analyzing data. Now the role is as a management consultant in a science that states: "Given these facts and this interpretation, I recommend this action." This does not, of course, mean that the action recommended will be pursued by management. Since the researcher is usually in a staff capacity, only recommendations can be offered. Management has the prerogative of accepting or rejecting the recommendations. However, the researcher must still recommend the action. Failure to do this is analogous to a dog chasing a car—the dog wouldn't know what to do with the car once he caught it.

The researcher should be involved in the problem definitions and objectives in order to be able to recommend courses of action based on interpretation of research results. To some, this approach may seem to be overstepping the researcher's responsibility to make recommendations, yet most managers appreciate this approach since it at least represents a starting point in deciding what action should be taken given certain results. Information has not really served its basic purpose until it is used in decision making. Techniques aimed at increasing the impact of the written and/or oral report are discussed in chapter 9.

MARKETING
INFORMATION SYSTEMS

Some organizations have moved beyond thinking of information needs in terms of projects and have focused their attention on creating *information systems* that provide a continuous flow of information to users. While such a focus may shift priorities in terms of the amount spent on information for a data base and that spent for specific projects, it should be pointed out that even if information is collected on a regular basis as a part of the information system, the principles of good marketing research set forth in this book are still applicable. The fact that information is collected on a regular basis does not negate the need for relating it to management decisions, for using correct sampling techniques, and so on. The basic principles—directly or indirectly—apply to all information flows. An understanding of these principles will help ensure better quality of information regardless of the nature of the system or procedures used to provide the information.

SUMMARY

This chapter has focused on the purpose, use, and overall approaches to gathering information for making marketing decisions. An understanding of the decision-making process, along with knowing how information can aid a manager, is the basis for planning and implementing research projects. Research projects should be carried out so that this focus of providing problem-solving information is central to the research process. This chapter outlined such an approach. Chapter 2 lays the framework for research as it relates to planning and strategic marketing decisions.

chapter two

Strategy Research
and the Planning Process

Years ago, the local country store served the product needs of an entire community. The typical country store-owners were aware of the individual needs of each member of their communities and based their purchasing and inventory on that knowledge. Today's marketplace has undergone enormous expansion since the day of the country store. Manufacturers, as well as retailers, are becoming increasingly further removed from the consumer public. Growth, changing needs, and increased competition necessitate a closer understanding between businesses and the customer or client base they serve. Research is designed to provide that link of understanding. Research is a tool through which businesses can obtain an accurate picture of a changing, growing marketplace. Few organizations are able to operate successfully without current and accurate information about their market environment. Marketing research, like the country store, has also experienced an evolution in scope, accuracy, and purpose. Information needs extend far beyond data-related sales projections. The customer and the prospective sector of the marketplace, corporate image concerns, product positioning goals, investor attitudes, buyer motivation factors, the competitive environment, and market demand forecasts have brought the role of research up into increasingly higher decision-making circles.

STRATEGY RESEARCH

The challenge in future business environments will be to operate successfully with competition at levels never before seen. The key to business success in this evolving competitive environment is planning. The key to planning is information. Accurate, reliable, and timely decision-making management information, designed as the foundation for the management planning process, is provided by strategy research. Whereas research in itself is the process of systematically gathering and evaluating information, strategy research is the integration of the tools and techniques of research, competitive analysis, and forecasting into the planning and decision process. The goal of strategy research, therefore, is to provide management with market strategy decision-making information.

STRATEGY RESEARCH, MANAGEMENT DECISIONS, AND THE PLANNING PROCESS

The need for management to anticipate the future is becoming increasingly more important in the decision-making process. Planning must consider the changing environment, the changing behavior of customers, the changing competitive forces, and the impact of these changes on current and future activities, but the key is understanding the impact that present decisions will have on future business environments. The truly successful business competitors of the future will be those who understand these dynamics and who can initiate and set the pace for market trends instead of merely reacting to changes in the business environment.

The strategic management process as defined as Philip Kotler is the managerial process of developing and maintaining a viable relationship between the organization and its environment through the development of corporate purpose, objectives and goals, growth strategies, and business portfolio plans for companywide operations. Strategy research is an integral part of this strategic management process. Strategy research serves to define and clarify existing and developing relationships between an organization and its environment. Understanding these relationships allows for prediction. The predictive results of strategy research are supplemented with updates of marketplace conditions. This process maximizes the information benefits by creatively utilizing both qualitative and quantitative methodologies that often employ a multifaceted approach in the design of a project.[1]

The purpose of planning is decision making. At the heart of the decision-making process is the reduction of errors in reasoning. The accuracy of the information and assumptions used in the planning process

14

therefore becomes vital. Errors in decision can result from fallacies in reasoning, which may in turn result from misinformation or lack of information. Research serves the essential role of reducing the error in decision making.

Alexander H. Cornell outlines sources of decision-making error. Decision-making error may result from the lack of problem formulation or inflexibility in considering new information. It is often the consequence of adherence to cherished beliefs or parochialism. Communication failure is another source of error in the decision process. Overemphasis on the model, excessive attention to detail, and failure to ask the right questions add to the potential for error. Likewise, incorrect use of information, disregard for the limitations of information results, concentration on statistical uncertainty, and inattention to uncertainties also enhance the possibility of inaccuracies, as can the use of side issues as criteria, neglect of subjective elements, or the failure to periodically reappraise assumptions and data. Each of these examples reflects either bias, a lack of utilization of proper information, or a misapplication of otherwise valid information. Strategy research, designed as an integral part of the planning and decision-making process, seeks to reduce the potential for bias, provide the necessary information, and ensure that the information is valid and properly utilized.[2]

The planning, decision making, and strategy research orientation assumes that short- and long-range planning of corporate activities must take place on a continuing basis. The consequence of the development of consistent strategies and tactics is an integrated system of corporate and marketing activities. These are vital to the strategic management process. This orientation also assumes that strategy research is utilized to arrive at more fact-founded decisions than might be derived from strictly intuitive approaches. Additionally, strategy research will aid in the very important role of developing goals and targets. A market potential orientation, rather than production goals, therefore becomes the primary guide to corporate action. The implications of departmental decisions are recognized and the goal of integrating all corporate and marketing strategy efforts is sought. This orientation seeks to promote a more systematic approach to product innovation in a climate that encourages innovation and creativity based on finely tuned feedback from a dynamic and changing market environment. New product planning and development are a natural outgrowth of this orientation and reflect an important emphasis in corporate policy. A marketing focus that coordinates company effort to accomplish corporate and departmental objectives consistent with company profit and growth objectives underlies this process. This includes the flexibility to reshape company products, services, and goals on a continuing basis to meet the demands and opportunities of the market environment. Finally, these elements and interrelationships undergo regular redefinition and refinement to systematize the discovery and implementation of corporate and marketing opportunity.[3]

PLANNING AND
THE OBJECTIVES OF DECISIONS

The requirement for decisions therefore underlies the planning process. Any rational and systematic approach to the decision process must reflect corporate or marketing objectives. The formulation of the decision problem evolves from the question of why a decision is necessary in the first place. The definition of the problem then becomes fundamental in the development of the objectives to be considered for any decision making. Most decision objectives are quantifiable. This quantitative analysis of the decision problem will involve measurement. Measurement allows for a numerical description of alternative strategies being considered by the decision objectives. This approach allows for several strategies to be effectively and systematically compared.[4]

THE PURPOSE OF RESEARCH

Whereas the requirement for decisions underlies the planning process, the purpose of research is *to reduce the error in decision making*. Research designs are developed to enable the decision maker to evaluate alternatives as objectively, accurately, and economically as possible. The research design is deliberately and specifically conceived and executed to bring empirical evidence, in the form of clearly defined and accurate market environment feedback, to bear on the problem. This is accomplished by setting up a framework for tests of the differences and relationships between variables. The reduction of decision-making error in strategy research extends to prediction. Prediction should not be confused with forecasting, but should precede and become the basis for forecasting. One predicts by establishing a valid relationship between two or more variables. By clearly defining any given set of variables and then applying appropriate measurement to examine the existence or nonexistence of any relationship, an outcome can be predicted. Reducing the error in decision making becomes the fundamental purpose for developing *decision-making information*. Strategy research is the tool with which decision-making information is accurately and systematically developed.

RETURN ON RESEARCH

All decisions involve risk. In most cases, money becomes a natural and early measure of the decision objective alternatives. Money thereby becomes an index for evaluating the relative degree of risk of various courses of action. Research, then, as an integral part of the planning and decision-making process, must be viewed as an investment. The investment accountability of research can be viewed in much the same way as that of manufacturing, sales, advertising, research and development, product development, and administration. The cost of research should be evaluated in light of the risk (by way of capital or assets) related to the decision or decisions under consideration. It then follows that the value of research is viewed within the context of the possible return on the investment.

Research has been defined as a source of systematically gathered and analyzed information. The value of research will always be directly related to the value of the information on which its results are based. The value of the information will depend on its accuracy. The probability of making a correct decision will be in direct relation to the accuracy of the information on which the decision is based. When properly designed and executed, strategy research can produce a return on investment that is as great as or greater than other corporate investment expenditures. However, if improperly used, designed, or directed, research can prove to be worthless and even misleading.

Properly designed and executed research requires the selection of the right type of research for a given planning and decision process. This selection should be based on a clear understanding of the objectives of the research as well as the ultimate value of the risk involved in the decision alternatives. The final cost of research is then evaluated in terms of the value of the decision involved and the potential return on investment expected as a result of reducing the potential for error in that decision.

DECISION-MAKING INFORMATION, PLANNING, AND FORECASTING

Any systematic decision making must take into account a knowledge of the existing situation or market environment to which the decision applies and the ways in which the situation or environment might change over time. Understanding the relationships between the variables or factors involved within this environment must undergird any effective forecasting. A limited or inaccurate knowledge of the present situation and how it might change over time will result in decisions based primarily on weak assumptions and uncertainty. This certainty increases the potential for risk in any decision process. Good forecasting involves a great deal more than just the skillful utilization of mathematical and statistical data to project the future. Good forecasting must also include an understanding of the market dynamics involved, competitive activity, current economic factors, the effects of outside events on timing and demand, and primary feedback relative to customer needs, preferences, motivations, and perceptions. Forecasts allow the decision maker to evaluate alternatives with respect to the future impact of present decisions.[5]

ENVIRONMENTS
OF UNCERTAINTY
AND OPPORTUNITY ASSESSMENT

As the business environment has become more competitive and global in scope, it has also become more uncertain. The planning and decision process has of necessity become a broader discipline involving all facets of the consumer-environment-firm interaction. The integration of planning, decision making, and research is certainly one result. Another is the integration and systematization of the various marketing functions with each other and with the other key functions of the business enterprise. These unified approaches, which are being taken together more and more with behavioral and quantitative techniques, serve as more realistic models of human and market behavior to aid in decision making and planning. These integrations are producing planning and decision processes that are more congruent with our technologically based information society. Managerial, technological, and consumer-societal-environmental dimensions are the vital parts comprising modern-day planning and decision making. Therefore, the knowledge of basic principles of management and marketing, human behavior, decision sciences, and the environment is used in conjunction with information technology and the overall strategy planning process. These integrated principles and processes serve to assess business and marketing opportunity, planning and programming of marketing activities, and the ongoing evaluation and adjustment of marketing effort.

The assessment of opportunity is one of the most important challenges faced by decision-making executives. The challenge is even more important in an environment wrought with flux and uncertainty. Anticipated changes in the environment must be analyzed and creatively related to the profitable use of corporate resources. Decisions determined from these assessments are then translated into policies and plans, which then give direction to the company in its efforts to adapt to its economic and environmental setting in order to achieve its corporate goals. The long-term view of resource adaptation in assessing opportunity recognizes that the most important factor in capitalizing on opportunity is not technological or financial, but conceptual. Information developed through strategy research must be used to identify and conceptualize needs that can be satisfied, to create new demands, to find new markets, and to serve them profitably.[6]

Assessing environmental change is one of the most important factors of decision-making information. The rate and magnitude of change and its effect on a firm will certainly have an impact on product innovation, the flow of new products, product positioning, and competitive strategies. Understanding change must be the basis for any assessment of market opportunity. Correct assessment of market opportunity requires the identification and analysis of relevant factors interacting within the market environment. The merging of the assessment of these factors to relevant resources of the firm and the needs of customers becomes the goal of the planning and decision process. Some of the important determinants that affect the assessment of opportunity and the formulation of marketing and competitive strategy include the accelerating rate of technological change based on new advances; changing lifestyles; rigorous domestic and foreign competition in all product areas; government influence and intervention in the private sector; changing concepts of marketing, communications, information processing and storage, organization, and management style; and trends toward concentration of power in larger companies in an environment of creative, innovative competition from smaller, entrepreneurial firms. The constant change within the market environment does create opportunities, but it also can reduce the attractiveness and future value of opportunities previously recognized. Therefore, an understanding of current environmental dynamics is a critical requisite for sound management of change, since opportunities evolve from these interactions.

Another very important aspect of evaluating change and identifying opportunity is the area of product planning. Many growth industries are built upon and sustained by an orderly and consistent flow of new products. But most products pass through stages of consumer acceptance known as the *product life cycle*. The product life cycle curve is explained by the phase on a new product/acceptance curve (see Figure 2.1). The first phase of the product acceptance curve involves the developing market. Those most inclined to make first use of the product during this phase are known as the *innovators*. Innovators are followed closely by *early adopters*. This phase is typified generally by slow growth. As awareness and product acceptance increase, the next phase is entered. This is a phase of increasingly faster growth and competition. Those customers who enter during this phase are known as the *pseudo-innovators*. They differ from the early adopters by lagging behind somewhat in acceptance simply to see how the product is accepted. The *majority* enter after the pseudo-innovators. Volume increases substantially at this point. The *late adopters* follow the majority in their acceptance of the new technology or product. Understanding product life cycle theory as it relates to environmental and opportunity assessment is very important. A product in the later stages of the life cycle curve, for example, may need to be modified to seek new markets and to identify key segments to focus on and target, or even possibly to be eliminated. This is done most effectively through timely and accurate feedback from the marketplace.[7]

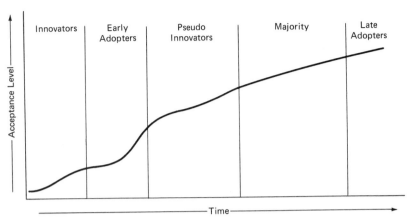

Innovators | Early Adopters | Pseudo Innovators | Majority | Late Adopters

Acceptance Level

Time

Figure 2.1

STRATEGY RESEARCH,
MARKETING PLANNING,
AND COMPETITIVE STRATEGY

Financial and production planning have long been practiced in business. Formal marketing planning, defined as the systematic attention to careful calculation and coordination of corporate means and marketing ends, is a relatively newer development. Formal marketing planning involves the definition of concrete marketing objectives and the program of action designed to achieve them. Flux in the market environment, technology advances, and increased competition have caused marketing planning to evolve from a management luxury to a process that is indispensable for the survival, growth, and profitable operation of a firm. Formal marketing planning has become an integrative process that blends corporate goals and resources with decision-making information on opportunities that have been identified. The object of this planning is to develop creative and innovative policies based on strategic information in order to guide corporate efforts into the marketplace.

Strategic thinking and planning are therefore finding a more prominent place in decision circles. Strategies are being spelled out in clearer terms for all aspects of planning. Alternatives and rationales for alternatives are being based on more incisive and accurate market feedback and competitive information. Kotler points out that a company's marketing strategy will consider the company's competitive size and position in the market environment; the company's resources, objectives, and policies; competitor marketing strategies; the target market's buying behavior; the stage of the product life cycle; and the character of the economy. A clear understanding of a company's market position is basic to developing effective competitive strategies. Kotler explains that in most situations a company will either be a market leader, a market challenger, a market follower, or a market nicher.[8]

The *market leaders* are those who occupy first place by way of market share for a particular type of product line. Market leaders seek to remain number one. Their goals are usually to expand total market usage of the product, to protect their current market share through good defensive and offensive strategies, and to expand market share. *Market challengers* are generally those firms occupying the second, third, or fourth place in market share. These firms are usually quite large in their own right. Market challengers also seek to gain market share. They attempt to accomplish this by frontal assault or flanking movement strategies against the market leaders. The flanking strategies are preferred since the concentration of effort is with greater strength against an area of weakness in the leader. Market challengers are also known to employ "guppy strategies," as defined by Kotler. Guppy strategies involve attacking smaller competitors rather than the market leader. *Market followers* seldom choose to make frontal or head-on attacks on market leaders. Market followers are in that category simply by virtue of their size relative to the other competition. Market followers usually can effectively employ flanking and guppy strategies in their competitive environment. *Market nichers* are smaller firms that operate in a particular segment of the market. Their strategies usually do not include head-on clashes with market leaders. Market nichers usually occupy an area of specialization that leaders tend to overlook or ignore.[9]

A firm's position as a market leader, challenger, follower, or nicher parallels some new concepts in competitive strategy known as *marketing warfare strategy*. Military leaders have been employing effective principles of strategy for centuries. Many of these principles are being adopted by major corporations for marketing plans and competitive strategies. In brief, market leaders occupy the high ground, or a defensive position. Market challengers are usually in an attack or offensive mode against the leader. Market followers can employ flanking strategies effectively. Market nichers are like guerrillas. They must be mobile and they always attack unexpectedly at points of weakness. Such attacks usually are also followed by hasty retreats.

Competitive strategy, therefore, begins with an understanding of a company's market position as a market leader, challenger, follower, or nicher. Once this is established, an understanding of how the firm is positioned in the minds of the customers in the marketplace is paramount. Returning to the concept of marketing warfare, the battleground is in the minds of the customers. Each competitive product will occupy a position in the minds of customers. That position involves the strengths and weaknesses of a firm relative to the competition, as perceived by the customers.

The final concept relating to strategy research, marketing planning, and competitive strategy is market segmentation. Whereas positioning reflects an understanding of how various competitors are perceived relative to one another in the minds of the customers, segmentation allows for the categorization of customers into subsets based on some type of shared characteristic or shared agreement about attitudes and/or lifestyles. Segmentation can be based on demographic characteristics, psychographic profiles, product preference/lifestyle profiles, geographic differences, or behavioristic profiles.

Effective competitive strategies, as a part of the overall planning process, are based on decision-making information that relates to market positions, product positioning, and market segmentation. Additionally, a clear understanding of the interrelationships among market position, product positioning, and market segments becomes the driving factor for effective competitive strategy planning.

SUMMARY

The challenge for a business's future will be successful operation in market environments wrought with change and increased intensities of competition. Accurate, reliable, and timely decision-making management information, designed as the foundation of the management planning process, has become an essential ingredient in achieving the competitive edge. Strategy research furnishes this decision-making information through the integration of the tools and techniques of research, competitive analysis, forecasting, and marketing strategy.

NOTES

1. PHILIP KOTLER, *Marketing Management* (Englewood Cliffs, N.J.: Prentice-Hall, 1980).

2. ALEXANDER H. CORNELL, *The Decision Maker's Handbook* (Englewood Cliffs, N.J.: Prentice-Hall, 1980).

3. EUGENE J. KELLEY, *Marketing Planning and Competitive Strategy* (Englewood Cliffs, N.J.: Prentice-Hall, 1972).

4. DAVID W. MILLER and MARTIN K. STARR, *Executive Decisions and Operations Research* (Englewood Cliffs, N.J.: Prentice-Hall, 1969).

5. KELLEY.

6. Ibid.

7. KOTLER.

8. Ibid.

9. Ibid.

chapter three

Strategic Research Designs for Decision Making

THE DECISION-MAKING PERSPECTIVE OF RESEARCH

Research has already been described as the process of systematically gathering and analyzing information. Strategy research is the integration of the tools and techniques of research, competitive analysis, and forecasting as an integral part of the planning and decision process. Whereas the goal of strategy research is to provide decision-making information for management, the purpose of any research is to reduce the error in decision making. Research, therefore, links an organization with its marketing environment. The specification, gathering, analyzing, and interpretation of decision-making information that will allow a clearer understanding of the environment, identify problems and opportunities, and develop and evaluate alternative courses of action for planning form the basic purpose of research. The inclusion of the specification and interpretation of necessary information as a part of the decision process is an important feature in defining research as an aid to decision making. "Research" is too commonly used within the narrow definition of simply gathering and analyzing data to pass on for interpretation and possible use.[1]

Strategy research begins within the context of the planning and decision process. Once research objectives are specified, the decision about what type of research design is to be developed and chosen must be made. The choice of design must reflect a keen understanding of the alternatives to be considered as well as the designs that will provide the best fit for the alternatives. Management, along with the research director and research consultant, must be involved in the inception stages. Likewise, the research director and research consultant should be interacting with management decision makers in interpreting the subtleties of the results and their impact on the decision alternatives.

THE RESEARCH PROCESS

The first step in the research process is reaching agreement on the purpose to be served by the particular research project within the context of the planning and decision process. This usually consists of identifying the decisions to be supported, the opportunities to be evaluated, or the environmental analysis to be defined or clarified. Once it is established, the research purpose is then translated into specific research objectives. An estimate of the value of the information and the return on the research investment is then made. The next step involves determining the research design that will best fit the information required. The research design will inolve the selection of research methodologies and sampling procedures, as well as outlining the structure and sequencing of the overall research project. The final step in the research process is implementing the design. This begins with designing the data-gathering instrument (questionnaire or discussion guide), followed by the collection, manipulation, and analysis of the data, and is completed with the interpretation of the data as they relate to the specific decision alternatives.

Research Designs and Strategies

The research design provides the blueprint for carrying out the research project. This blueprint is formulated around a structure based on the decision alternatives that relate to the problems or opportunities to be assessed. The research strategy chosen will depend first on an evaluation of the cost-benefit or return on research expected. This will determine how extensive the design must be. In some instances, secondary data and information available from the internal corporate information system will be appropriate to the decisions being considered. In most cases, however, a review of secondary and internal existing data is an important first step. Qualitative research may be the next step. It may be the only step when only a preliminary or exploratory investigation is necessary. Examples of qualitative research include expert opinion interviews, depth interviews, and focus group interviews. Quantitative research may be the next phase of the research or it may incorporate the basic thrust of the research by itself. Quantitative research will use a survey method, observational methods, or causal research experimentation. The research project strategy serves to ensure that the approach taken to develop the decision-making information will provide the optimum fit and evaluation for alternatives being considered in the decision and planning process.

Although the research design itself may specify the use of very rigorous scientific tools, preparing the research project will depend heavily upon the creativity and ingenuity of the research designer. The expertise and experience of the research designer becomes pivotal in formulating meaningful, custom-tailored research designs for particular decision-making information needs. The research design, therefore, is at the heart of the research strategy, as well as the planning strategy. The research design provides the research plan of action; specifies sources of data; outlines the methodology and statistical procedures; details available resources; sets the schedule for the research; and defines the problem and objectives of the research study. The research design, then, consists of the plan, the structure, and the strategy for developing the decision-making information and reducing the likelihood of error in the decision process because of the accuracy and pertinence of the information.[2]

Objectives of Research

There are three primary objectives that a research project can accomplish. A proper understanding and utilization of these three objectives must undergird any effective research design plan. When long-range plans are involved or when the decision alternatives represent very sizable investments, all three of the basic objectives should be satisfied in the research project. When the risk or investment that will result from the decision is minimal, then a research design focused on the first or second objective may satisfy the information needs. The first objective of research is *to identify the variables*. The second objective is *to determine the differences between the variables*. The third research objective is *to establish the relationships existing between the variables*.

The objective of identifying the variables ensures that no essential ingredients are neglected. This phase of research is usually exploratory or qualitative in nature. It involves an examination of what needs to be studied. This objective may be satisfied by expert opinion interviews, depth interviews, and/or focus group interviews. This first objective greatly reduces the likelihood that a major report will conclude with results recommending further study because something was overlooked.

The second objective of research is the one with which most people are familiar. Determining the differences between variables—whether they are attitudes, purchase preferences, or some other factor—is simply a percentage analysis of responses given in a survey. A certain percentage of the population will feel one way, another percentage will see things another way, and other groups will hold to other viewpoints. The bottom line of any meaningful research is learning what differences make a

difference. This second objective includes simple percentage (or frequency) analysis as well as cross breaks. *Cross breaks,* which are also
known as cross tabulations, are simply more detailed percentage analyses
of responses (toward preferences, buying patterns, or so on), which are
categorized according to demographic, geographic, or other pertinent
subgroups of the total responses. Determining the differences between
the variables provides a "snapshot" of the marketplace at any given time.

The third objective of research—determining the relationships
between the variables—is the least understood and, probably, the most
overlooked or misused. Variables such as attitudes, buying preferences,
and motivational factors do not exist within any individual person or group
of persons totally independent from one another. Attitudes are interrelated and interdependent upon one another. The hot charcoals from a
grill burn with a different intensity when they are measured within the
context of the heat of the grill and the surrounding charcoals, when
compared to how they burn if measured by themselves outside the
context of the grill and other charcoals. Attitudes interrlate in a similar
fashion. The second objective of research analyzes each piece of charcoal
outside the grill. This is important and necessary. But the third objective
of research serves to evaluate the charcoals within the context of the grill.
The third objective of research will identify relationships between variables that have far greater significance than the individual variables have
by themselves. A variable that is mediocre in importance when viewed
by itself may become a pivotal factor on which a subgroup of variables
depends. Because this third research objective identifies the relationships
between variables, it is predictive in nature. Statistical methodologies
used for this objective may be designed to uncover emerging trends or
describe consumer-product lifestyle profiles. Methodologies for this
objective range from simple correlations to various forms of multiple
variable (multivariate) statistical procedures, including factor analysis,
multiple regression, discriminant analysis, and perceptual mapping.

Measurement, Methodology, and Design

A research project design involves the selection of a methodology from
which evaluation and measurement of data might yield the most appropriate manipulation of data. The measurement and manipulation of data
become key factors in formulating the end result of the decision-making
information sought. Measurement involves the assignment of numbers to
attitudes, behavior, or happenings according to rules. These rules relate
to the evaluative consistency of the systematic procedure served by the
statistical procedure utilized.[3]

There are four basic levels of measurement, which measure the two
basic types of variables—continuous and categorical. A variable is simply

a symbol to which numbers or values are assigned. *Continuous variables* have an ordered set of values within a certain range (one through ten). *Categorical variables* are classified into categories or subsets.

Variables in measurement are also termed as independent or dependent variables. An *independent variable* is the presumed cause of the *dependent variable,* which is the presumed effect. The level of frequency in radio listenership (independent variable) might presume certain listening preferences (dependent variables). This would be a case for measurement.

The four levels of variable measurement are nominal, ordinal, interval, and ratio measures. *Nominal measurement* amounts to little more than counting the number of objects in a subset of data. *Ordinal measures* involve ranking by size or rank-ordering measurements. *Interval measures* are numerically equal in distance from each interval in the characteristics being measured. A *ratio scale* is a special kind of interval measurement that has a meaningful zero point. Demographic categories, such as sex, occupation, or geographic location, are nominally scaled variables. A class standing or market share ordering would be an example of the ranking of characteristics of objects in an ordinal scale. Interval scaling is used extensively in attitude measurement. The increments between the numbers used to rank objects will be equal to those between intervals of the attribute being measured. A very wide range of statistical procedures can be employed to measure variables using interval scaling. Measuring the importance of product attributes on a scale from no importance at all to extreme importance is an example.[4]

Decisions concerning the market environment are usually based on an understanding of customer behavior and an ultimate desire to influence that behavior. The measurement of attitudes provides indicators and explanations for behavior. Attitudes are basically mind-sets used as parameters from which the environment is perceived. They are guides indicating how consumers will respond to the environment. Attitudes are composed of important components. The first is a person's cognitions or knowledge about an object or situation. This component usually focuses on awareness measures. Awareness levels precede evaluative beliefs, which become the bases for judgments about characteristics and attributes inherent in an object. Attribute judgments might require comparisons of different products.

Another component of attitudes involves feelings toward a situation, object, or person. Comparative judgments of liking or disliking something are standard forms of measurement for this component. Still another component of attitudes involves a person's expectations of how they will respond to an object in the future; this is the *intentions* component. For example, this might involve the likelihood that someone will purchase a particular object or brand. Each component of attitudes builds upon the other. This is known as the *hierarchy of effects of attitudes,* which orders the components hierarchically, beginning with cognitions or knowledge and ending with behavior.[5] The premise follows that a change in one component only takes place after a change in the preceding components. A change in intentions, therefore, would follow an increase in awareness and a change in preference for the objects or products in question.

For measuring attitudes, rating scales such as constant sum scales, paired comparisons, rank order scales, and summated scales are most commonly used. *Constant sum scales* would be used in the determination of market share where all purchases of a particular product would total 100 percent. *Paired comparisons* involve consumer choice between paired products. *Rank order scales* can serve a diversity of measurement needs, from measuring the importance of product attributes to measuring preference for particular brands of different products. *Summated scales* are interval scales. The most popular are Likert scales, which also have a variety of potential applications. Likert scales can measure degree of agreement, liking, preference, likelihood of purchase, and so on.[6]

These measurement techniques are combined with a variety of statistical procedures, each of which is designed to address different decision questions. The most basic statistical procedures are frequency (percentage) analyses and mean (average) score analyses. Tests such as chi squares are used to measure significance in the differences between categorical type variables. Other analyses test the relationship between variables. Examples of these analyses would be correlations, Spearman rho, regression analysis, factor analysis, cluster analysis, discriminant analysis, multidimensional scaling, perceptual mapping, semantic differential, and conjoint analysis. There are many other techniques, but these are the most widely used.

The interesting fact about the more sophisticated analytic techniques is the simplicity of their results. Most of the techniques just mentioned require a computer program for timely execution. Yet the bottom line of their usefulness is that they take very complex issues (such as a myriad of seemingly conflicting attitudes in the minds of a large group of people) and reduce them to basic, meaningful, and understandable drivers or indicators.

Some of the basic questions addressed by these key analytic techniques include:

1. *Regression analysis*—What variables are predictive of changes in consumer attitudes and behavior? How can response and stimulus be quantitatively related?
2. *Discriminant analysis*—What are the real differences among market segments, products, and concepts?
3. *Factor analysis*—How can data be reduced to their underlying entities through logical, objective combinations of characteristics or respondents? Can profiles of customers be formulated that relate to product preference (or motivational appeals) and consumer lifestyles?

4. *Cluster analysis*—Can meaningful market segments be defined and described for more effective targeting of a product or service?

5. *Conjoint measurement*—What trade-offs does a consumer make in buying or evaluating a product or service? How important are such give-and-take considerations to each other and to the overall selection process?

6. *Perceptual mapping and multidimensional scaling*—How can a complex set of interrelating characteristics be reduced to understandable attributes associated with brands or companies by means of a two-dimensional spatial plot? How are products, services, brands, companies, or concepts perceived and described relative to one another? (Perceptual mapping is one of the strongest tools now being used in studies involving positioning or repositioning of products, services, brands, or companies.)

CONSUMER
AND COMMUNICATIONS
RESEARCH PERSPECTIVES

Learning what differences among consumers make a difference underlies th basic purpose of research, which is the reduction of error in decision making. Determining the differences that make a difference also implies establishing similarities among consumers. All this involves learning as much about the customer as possible. What are the habits, lifestyles, attitudes, and buying preferences of customers? How do they differ and how are they similar? Effectively reaching target markets to influence behavior implies an understanding of how the markets are defined and what makes them tick. Market segmentation will become increasingly important as competition levels increase. Understanding the factors that influence purchase decisions among clearly identified market segments, for example, will allow for more effective strategic targeting of messages to influence behavior as well as product development that reflects actual needs.

Obtaining demographic data has traditionally been the first step in segmentation. Education level, age, marital status, and geographic location will all provide useful information about differences among consumers. However, demographic data usually tell little about consumer feelings, awareness, or intentions toward products, services, or brands.

Demographic information, therefore, allows responses to individual research questions to be viewed by each demographic subsegment (such as age or income categories). However, segmentation cannot stop at this point. Psychographics and lifestyles pick up where demographics leave off.[7] Psychographics and lifestyle profiles may develop and become segments that are not clearly defined by demographic characteristics and are therefore more subtle and much more important for effective targeting. At other times, psychographic profiles and demographic characteristics complement each other. Psychographics and lifestyles include a whole range of personal attributes dealing with activities, interests, opinions, and habits. Research designs have been developed to illustrate the inter-relationships among product preferences and appeals, key demographic characteristics such as age and income, and lifestyle and psychographic attributes. These segmentation profiles provide added depth for understanding the dynamics of marketplaces in which effective targeting and positioning are becoming more subtle and are offering an increasingly greater challenge.

INDUSTRIAL
RESEARCH PERSPECTIVE

Developing research designs for industrial studies uses the same basic tools and procedures as for consumer studies. The attitude-to-behavior sequence is just as valid for industrial purchases as it is for consumer purchases. However, developing an industrial research design must usually be preceded by an understanding of the dynamics and subtleties of the particular sector of the marketplace to be studied. For example, the requirements of purchase decision makers might vary widely depending on whether they are at the end or the beginning of a budget cycle. In many cases, identifying and qualifying actual decision makers is a subtle process. There are specifying, recommending, and final authority decision makers. Final decision makers often merely approve what has been recommended. Purchasing agents will have full purchase authority for some items, yet for others they must adhere to strict guidelines set forth by engineering or operations staffs. Likewise, the differences in the size and type of respondent firms will be significant. These differences must be either properly categorized (to ensure that oranges are not compared to apples) or given fitting evaluatory emphasis. Segmentation among industrial research studies, therefore, might include geographic segmentation, end-use segmentation, buyer description segmentation, or specific product segmentation. End-use segmentation examples might be downhole oilfield equipment for use on deep land gas wells, or offshore flowing oilwells. Buyer description segments from the same industry might be major oil companies, large independent oil companies, or drilling contractors. Specific product segment examples might be rock bits, journal bits, or diamond drilling bits.

Very often, industrial study designs not only reflect the attitudes of industry decision makers, but also make evaluations of the trends and dynamics occurring within a particular sector of industry. The evaluations of market dynamics and trends frequently precede forecast assessments.

FORECASTING
AND PREDICTIVE DESIGNS

It has already been noted that prediction is different from and precedes forecasting. Prediction is an important component and should form the basis for any forecast. Prediction serves to identify the existence of a relationship between two or more variables. As such, prediction allows for the estimation of the present value of a variable or variables. Forecasting is the assignment of an estimate of future value to a variable or variables based on those cause-and-effect relationships.[8] There are four basic categories of forecast methodologies: qualitative techniques, cross-impact analysis, time-series analysis and projection methods, and causal modeling.[9]

Forecasts begin with the assumption that a relationship exists between the variable being forecast and one or more other variables that can be measured or estimated. The variable being forecast is the dependent variable and the others are the independent, explanatory, or determinant variables. This assumption of most forecasts is that the relationship between the variables will remain relatively stable over time, or will alter only in a way that can be anticipated. This assumption is usually the weakest link in any forecast. The third assumption underlying forecasts is that the relationship between the variables can be approximated, manipulated, and managed through various mathematical or statistical forms. This assumption holds only for the more rigorous methods of prediction and forecasting.[10]

Qualitative Techniques

Qualitative techniques are used most often when background data are lacking. This might include instances where there is no relevant history, in the case of a new product or technology, or when there simply is no good information about a particular subject area.

Delphi Method. There are different variations of Delphi techniques. Each, however, focuses on the opinions of experts in a given field. The most frequently used form of Delphi seeks to gain consensus of a group of experts on an uncertain matter. The experts are interviewed individually and are then provided with anonymous feedback information from other participants, allowing them to respond to divergent views, until patterns of shared agreement emerge. The Delphi techniques with the most potential involve personal interviews with authorities who possess an expert viewpoint on a particular subject area in common. To be most effective, the sample of authorities can be drawn from a variety of disciplines. For example, in the area of office products, the experts might include trade publication editors, technological experts, economists, communication policy experts, work force/worker morale authorities, social trends analysts, and marketing experts. Evaluations of shared agreement among subsets of experts in the sample are made and then compared with each subset category. This type of Delphi employs open-ended discussion guides rather than structured questionnaires. This allows for maximum depth and probing in the individual area of expertise for each expert before evaluating and comparing areas of shared agreement among the total group.

Social Trends Forecasts. Adaptations of product forecasts and attitudinal research have been combined to develop various methodologies used to identify and project social trends. One of the most penetrating methods involves sampling key trend-setting areas around the United States and conducting a content analysis of the newspaper headlines from local tabloids. This process has been refined by the Naisbitt Group. The technique has been used not only to track and project social trends but also to project their impact on various sectors of industry. Other techniques involve sampling opinion leaders or subregions that have been identified as trend-setters.

Expert Panel. This is in fact another form of Delphi. A panel of experts agree to participate in several rounds of a mail questionnaire or discussion guide. Before each round, each participant receives a copy of the results from the previous round. Another similar forecasting method is known as the *expert opinion focus group*. Six to ten experts are recruited to participate in a moderated, structured procedure that takes advantage of the dynamics and interaction of the group to probe and stimulate the discussion.

Historical Analogy. This method is based on the assumption that trends under similar circumstances will follow similar growth patterns.

Cross-Impact Analysis

This procedure is proving to be one of the more promising methods for medium- and long-range forecasting. It is simply a combination of techniques such as Delphi, expert panels or groups, and market research techniques. It ensures that proper identification of key factors is made, allows for the evaluation of the differences and relationships between those factors, and then assigns levels of importance, probabilities of occurrence, and the mutual interactions that exist between the factors.

Market Research Techniques. Market research techniques provide valuable input for forecasts only when *good* market research is performed.

Unfortunately, however, market research that is improperly directed or interpreted is too often biased and incomplete. Misinterpretation of findings and drawing wrong conclusions from the research are very possible when the research does not fulfill the requirements served by the three basic purposes of research, even if it is well executed. Strong interactions may exist between market variables that are simply not evident from visual examination of data that involves simple statistical analyses. This is where the third purpose of research, to determine the relationships between the variables, becomes critical. Several powerful statistical procedures already discussed (factor analysis, multiple regression, perceptual mapping, and so on) can provide important forecast input when properly designed. Good, objective market research can result in high accuracy levels for short-term forecasts (up to one year) and reasonable accuracy for intermediate forecasting (one to two years), but it becomes increasingly less accurate for long-range forecasts (three to ten years). Cross-impact analysis, combining a Delphi method with an in-depth research procedure reflecting feedback from the market environment, would greatly enhance the accuracy of long-range forecasts.

Time-Series Analysis and Projection Methods

Time-series analysis and projection methods may be used for the basis of forecasts when several years of data for a product are available and when relationships and trends tend to be relatively clear and stable. The *moving average* is probably the most frequently used time-series technique. This is simply a tracking of average scores (sales volumes, industry activity indicators, or other leading indicators) over consecutive points in time. These historical trends are usually tracked over two- to five-year time periods.

Exponential smoothing is a moving average procedure that gives more weight to recent data points in formulating the projected results. This technique can be effectively used in stable environments for short- to medium-range forecasts.

The *Box-Jenkins method* of forecasting merges time-series projections with other special knowledge, such as causal relationships. This method determines what lengths of moving average should be used and the weights to be assigned to past history, as well as other causal and definition parameters that provide the input for the model. Better results are obtained when several years of history are used.[11]

Trend projection procedures fit a trend line to a mathematical equation and then project the trend line into the future. Trend line projection is most commonly applied to annual data with at least five or more data points (years, for example). Trend line projections are valid only in very stable market environments.

Product acceptance curves are similar to product life cycle curves. Product acceptance curves provide an effective tool for evaluating projections of future growth levels for new products or new areas of technology. Product acceptance curves have been used very effectively in conjunction with Delphi techniques.

Causal Modeling

Causal models are very effective when historical data are available and sufficient analysis can be performed to effectively evaluate relationships between the factor to be forecast and other elements that will affect the forecast (related businesses, socioeconomic factors, and so on). Causal models mathematically express the relevant causal relationships. They may also include pertinent historical data and market research results. Causal models include regression models, econometric models, intentions to buy surveys, leading indicator models, and life cycle analysis. Regression models relate factors to be predicted (such as sales) to other elements of the system that explain their variation (economic, competitive, or internal variables). Econometric models involve a system of interdependent regression equations that describe a sector of activity to be predicted.[12]

Forecasting has been defined by Chester R. Wasson as "the art of making maximum use of available knowledge to derive a set of probabilities concerning future events."[13] Harry D. Wolfe outlines the following steps in forecasting:

1. Obtain adequate and accurate benchmark data.
2. Develop the data properly.
3. Utilize more than one forecasting method for the data.
4. Apply sound professional judgment and intuition to the forecasts.[14]

In conclusion, there should always be an awareness of the level on which the forecast is made. A full-scale forecast will begin with a forecast for the economy. If this is not feasible, then economic assumptions must be made as the basis of the forecast. The next step is to make the forecast for the industry or technology. This is followed by company forecasts and/or individual product line forecasts.

SUMMARY

The research design is the blueprint for systematically developing and assessing decision-making information to be used in the planning process. The research design involves the selection of research and forecasting methodologies that best fit alternatives to be considered. Understanding the three primary objectives of research helps in making a meaningful choice of procedures on which the design is based. Establishing the relationships that exist between variables is a primary requirement for providing an informational foundation for forecasting. The development of strategy research designs then combine the right choice of research, statistical, and forecasting procedures to formulate the basis for the planning and decision-making information required.

NOTES

1. DAVID A. AAKER and GEORGE S. DAY, *Marketing Research: Private and Public Sector Dimensions* (New York: John Wiley, 1980).

2. Ibid.

3. FRED N. KERLINGER, *Foundations of Behavioral Research* (New York: Holt, Rinehart and Winston, 1973).

4. JOSEPH F. HAIR, JR., ROLPH E. ANDERSON, RONALD L. TATHAM and BERNIE J. GRABLOWSKY, *Multivariate Data Analysis with Readings* (Tulsa: Penwell Publishing Company, 1979).

5. AAKER and DAY.

6. Ibid.

7. STEPHEN BAKER, *Systematic Approach to Advertising Creativity* (New York: McGraw-Hill, 1979).

8. WALTER B. WENTZ, *Marketing Research: Management and Methods* (New York: Harper & Row, Pub., 1972).

9. JOHN C. CHAMBERS, SATINDER K. MULLICK, and DONALD D. SMITH, *An Executive's Guide to Forecasting* (New York: John Wiley, 1974).

10. WENTZ.

11. CHAMBERS, et al.

12. Ibid.

13. CHESTER R. WASSON, *The Strategy of Marketing Research* (New York: Appleton-Century-Crofts, 1964).

14. HARRY D. WOLFE, *Business Forecasting Methods* (New York: Holt, Rinehart and Winston, 1966).

chapter four

Introduction to Data Collection

It is often stated that "the key to success is planning, and the key to good planning is proper information." Another variation of that theme is to say that "information is power." The success of all types of organizations in the final decades of the twentieth century will depend on the use of appropriate and strategic information. As indicated in earlier chapters, sound marketing decisions will depend on well-designed market research. In turn, even well-designed research must rely on the gathering of pertinent facts, figures, and other data directly related to the problems facing management. In earlier chapters we discussed the process of decision making and the importance of research design. Research design focuses on the overall framework or methodology for the collection and analysis of data in the marketing research process. Whether the research design is exploratory, descriptive, or experimental, its basic purpose will always be to gather useful information that can be classified, compared, and analyzed in relation to the original problem that initiated the research process. Data analysis and interpretation will be discussed in chapter 8. That chapter will deal with the process of taking the mass of raw data generated by the data collection process, and will show how to organize it into a format that answers the research question.

This section will deal specifically with the various types of data, the sources of data, the methods of data collection, and the procedures and tactics of data collection.

SOURCES OF DATA

A wide variety of data sources should be considered in answering the basic research question under consideration. The widely publicized "data explosion" will become worse if data collection does not focus on the research design and the original research question. Many people feel that quantity of data is the most important part of research. However, the research process must generate the data that can be translated properly into pertinent information that can be used to answer the specific question posed by the decision maker.

In order to quickly focus on the pertinent data relative to a research question, researchers and decision makers alike should be familiar with the basic sources of information related to the market under consideration. This will ensure that time and money are not wasted in a misdirected search for either unavailable or irrelevant information.

TYPES OF DATA

Generally, data are classified as (1) primary data, or (2) secondary data. *Primary data* are those data that have been collected for the first time by the researcher for the specific research project at hand. *Secondary data* are data already gathered by someone other than the researcher or data already existing in some form or another. There is some confusion about primary and secondary data because this classification has nothing to do with the relative importance of the information. Whether the data are primary or secondary is often determined by whether or not they were originated by the specific study in consideration.

The first commandment of data gathering is to exhaust all sources of secondary data before engaging in a search for primary data. Many research questions can be answered more quickly and with less expense through the proper use of secondary information. However, caution must be used to ensure that primary sources of secondary data are used since they are generally more accurate and complete than secondary sources.

Secondary Data

Since "the beginning is a very good place to begin," we will discuss the sources of secondary data first. The first problem that confronts a researcher in initiating a secondary data search is the massive amount, wide variety, and many locations of secondary data. Some method of logically summarizing the sources of secondary data is helpful. Most textbooks on the subject divide secondary data sources into two groups, (1) internal data sources, and (2) external data sources.

Internal secondary data sources are closest at hand since they are found within the organization initiating the research process. These internal data have been collected for other purposes but are available to be consolidated, compared, and analyzed to answer the research question. This is particularly true of organizations with sophisticated management information systems that routinely gather and consolidate useful marketing, accounting, and production information.

Specific internal records or sources of internal secondary data are:

1. Invoice records
2. Income statements (various cost information)
3. Sales results
4. Advertising expenditures
5. Accounts receivable logs
6. Inventory records
7. Production reports and schedules
8. Complaint letters and other customer correspondence
9. Salespeople's reports (observations)
10. Management reports
11. Service records
12. Accounts payable logs
13. Budgets
14. Distributor reports and feedback

Even though most research projects require more than just internal data, this is a very good place to begin the data search. Quite often a logical review of all internal secondary data sources will inexpensively give direction for the next phase of data collection. The internal search will give clues to what external data sources are required to gather the data base to create the information needed to answer the research question.

External secondary data sources are found outside the confines of the organization. There is an overwhelming number of external sources of data available to the reseacher. Hundreds of thousands of books and magazines are published each year while the government at all levels produces tens of thousands of annual reports and publications. Some of the more frequently used sources of secondary data are:

1. Government agencies and reports
2. Census data
3. Trade association reports
4. Books, periodicals, and newspapers
5. Dissertation abstracts
6. Annual reports
7. Syndicated commercial information
   a. Moody's
   b. Standard and Poor's

    c. A. C. Nielsen
    d. Market Research Corporation of America (MRCA)
8. *Annual Survey of Buying Power*
9. Standardized marketing data sources

Appendix B gives a more comprehensive list of data sources.

Your Local Library. One source that should never be overlooked is your local library, particularly if it is a federal depository. A well-equipped library will not only contain many of the sources mentioned above and in appendix B, but it will also have a variety of helpful indexes, directories, abstracts, and personnel who can assist in locating specific information. Any thorough search for secondary data should include a comprehensive library search. Various institutions also maintain excellent libraries in their areas of specializaion. Research foundations, financial institutions, energy companies, engineering firms, utilities, universities, and manufacturing concerns often maintain good libraries.

Uses of Secondary Data

There are several important uses of secondary data even though the research design might require the use of primary data. The most common uses of secondary data are summarized as follows:

1. In some cases the information and insights gained from secondary research are sufficient to answer the research question.
2. Secondary research can provide the background necessary to understand the problem and provide an overview of the market dynamics.
3. Secondary research can often provide exploratory information that can aid in the planning and design of the instruments used to gather primary information.
4. Secondary research can serve as a check and standard for evaluating primary data.
5. Secondary data can give insight into sample selection.
6. Secondary research can determine research hypotheses or ideas that can be studied in the primary data phase of the research process.

The extensive use of secondary data reduces the possibility of "reinventing the wheel" by gathering primary data that someone else has already collected.

Advantages of Secondary Data

Secondary data are gathered for some purpose other than the research project at hand. Consequently, researchers must understand and appreciate the relative advantages and disadvantages of secondary information. To properly use and evaluate secondary information, its value must be assessed. Secondary data possess the following advantages:

1. *Low cost.* The relatively low cost of secondary data is one of the most attractive characteristics. The cost of these data is very low when they are obtained from published sources. There is no design cost, and only the cost of the time required to obtain them is incurred. Even when the secondary information is provided by a commercial firm, it is normally less expensive than primary data because it is available on a multiclient basis rather than being custom designed on a proprietary basis.
2. *Speed.* A secondary data search can be accomplished much more quickly than can primary data collection, which requires design and execution of a primary data collection instrument.
3. *Exclusivity.* Some information is available only in the form of secondary data. For example, census information is available only in secondary form. Some types of personal and financial data cannot be obtained on a primary basis.
4. *Flexibility.* Secondary data are flexible and provide great variety.

Disadvantages of Secondary Data

Since secondary data, both internal and external, were generated for some purpose other than to answer the research question at hand, care must be taken in their application. The limitations of secondary data must be considered. Secondary data have the following potential limitations or disadvantages:

1. *A poor "fit."* The secondary data collected for some other research objective or purpose may not be relevant to the research question at hand. In most cases the secondary data will not fit the problem. In other cases secondary data collected from various sources will not be in the right intervals, units of measurement, or categories for proper cross-comparison.
2. *Questionable accuracy.* The question of accuracy takes several things into consideration. First, there is the question of whether the secondary data came from a primary source or a secondary source. Secondary sources of secondary data should be avoided. The next consideration is the organization or agency that originally collected the data. What is the quality of their methodology and data-gathering design? What is their reputation for credibility?
3. *Age.* A major problem with published and secondary data is the timeliness of the information. Old information is not necessarily bad information; however, in many dynamic markets up-to-date information is absolutely necessary.
4. *Quality.* The quality of the secondary information is sometimes unknown.

Secondary Data Summary

Whenever research requirements are defined, secondary data should be exploited first to give background, direction, and control over the total research process. Beginning with a secondary data search will ensure that the maximum benefit is derived from the collection of primary data. All pertinent secondary data should be gathered before moving to the primary gathering stage, because it is generally quicker and cheaper to collect secondary data. Good secondary data can be found both internally and externally. Library facilities should be used as a starting point in gathering secondary data; the federal government is the largest single source of secondary information.

While secondary information may answer the research question, generally it provides only the springboard for a collection of specific custom-designed information.

PRIMARY DATA

While some research questions can be resolved by the use of secondary data, many research projects require the collection of primary data. Primary data are generated in a research project for a specific purpose in a specific format and collected from a specific population sample. Depending on the research design there are various requirements for primary data and methods of collecting it. As mentioned earlier, the place to begin the data collection process is with a thorough review of secondary data.

Primary data have not been collected previously or gathered for any previous project. Some of the major sources of this type of information are:

1. *The organization itself*. We generally think of the organization as a source of internal secondary information; however, the organization can also be a valuable beginning source of primary data for answering research problems.
2. *The environment*. The market environment includes customers, potential customers, and competition. Customers are very important sources of information about their demands and intentions. Knowledge about potential customers is also an important element for any market research project. An emerging factor relative to the market environment is the competition. This factor is increasing in importance, and the next decade will bring severe marketing warfare among competitors. Information can be gathered from customers and even potential customers much more easily than from the competition. It is difficult to obtain information directly from competitors; however, other competitive analysis is an important part of a research project and requires primary data.
3. *The distribution channel*. Wholesalers, retailers, manufacturers, and various suppliers and users can be vital sources of information for an organization.

TYPES OF PRIMARY DATA

There are many types of primary data. They can be classified as data that answer "who," "what," and "why" questions. The "who" questions are answered by demographic characteristics and, to some extent, psycho-graphic characteristics. *Demographic characteristics* include such items as the respondents' educational level, age, sex, marital status, income, ethnic group, occupation, and social status. These variables can be used to identify who is likely to buy various products, read certain publications, or attend different events. *Psychographic characteristics* are measures of respondents' attitudes and measure such things as trend setting, risk taking, propensity to use credit, propensity to consume, and many other attitudes. This type of information can produce consumer profiles that are effective in identifying market segments.

The "what" questions are answered by purchase inventory questions and questions related to activities and behavior. The "why" questions are answered by research into consumer motivation. Attitude research can also provide insight into the reasons and opinions behind certain behavior patterns.

METHODS OF COLLECTING
PRIMARY DATA

The study design of any research project is developed to meet the objec-tives of the study. This research design will call for specific types of information and, also, specific methods of gathering the data. The primary methods of collecting primary data are (1) communication, and (2) obser-vation. *Communication* includes various ways to ask questions directly of respondents by personal interview, telephone survey, or mail question-naire. *Observation* involves viewing market situations either in the field or in a laboratory setting. In this method an observer records predeter-mined activities of the entity being observed. Sometimes the actions of interest are recorded by mechanical devices instead of by the observer. Observations in a laboratory setting are generally considered to be of causal design and experimental in nature.

Procedures of
the Communication Method

Communication is the most commonly used approach to gathering pri-mary data. Interviewing is used so frequently because it is a flexible way to gather information about people—their actions, attitudes, and inten-tions. Communication includes personal interviews, telephone surveys, and mail questionnaires. In most cases communication survey research involves the use of a questionnaire or discussion guide. The specific type of survey method should match the information requirements of the study design.

There are three basic interviewing methods. Each method may be used to implement many different types of surveys. The method to be employed and the type of survey to be conducted are determined by the problem that is to be solved and the various interviewing techniques or sampling considerations that will be necessary in order to solve the problem. The three basic methods are (1) personal, (2) telephone, and (3) mail.

Personal Interviewing. This face-to-face method is employed when the survey may be too long to conduct over the telephone or when there is material to show the respondent. Personal interviews are effective when the interviewer is placing a product, when the respondent is testing a product, and when the sample necessitates contacting homes in a specific manner (such as going to every fourth home or going to every home until an interview is conducted, and then skipping a specified number of homes before attempting the next contact), as well as other applications. Personal interviewing allows for more in-depth probing on various issues. There are several varieties of personal interviews. The most common are discussed below.

• In door-to-door interviewing, the client or field service director will assign an interviewing location and often the exact address at which to begin. The interviewer takes a specific direction in order to contact respondents according to the sample pattern that is to be followed. The interviewer will ask the questions and record the respondents' answers either during the interview or immediately afterward.

• Central location or mall interviewing is effective in many tests where a respondent will taste a product, look at a package design, view a commercial, or listen to a recording and report his or her impressions. Shopping centers are generally used because the high volume of traffic provides many prospective respondents. Several respondents may view a commercial, listen to a recording, or participate in a taste test at the same time, after which they are interviewed individually. When this method of interviewing is used, several interviewers work as a team. A central location, such as a church meeting hall or other facility, might be used to conduct a large number of personal interviews. When this method is used, the respondents are generally recruited in advance, either over the phone or at a mall intercept facility.

• Vendor/dealer/executive/professional interviewing can also be conducted on the telephone, but it is done face-to-face when it is necessary to probe deeply about specific information. An interview with an expert in a particular area is an excellent way to produce exploratory information. This information can then be used to form the basis of questionnaire design. Good background and exploratory research leads to good questionnaire design, which in turn leads to good descriptive research.

• Depth or focus group interviewing is normally an unstructured person-to-person interview or dicussion that allows the subjects to talk freely about their attitudes toward specific topics. A general discussion guide is usually followed, and in some cases an actual questionnaire is filled out. The depth interview allows for careful probing that will lead to very deep responses by the subject. Consequently, depth interviewing can lead to the collection of a greater "depth" of information, opinion, or feeling than can other types of interviews.

A focus group interview is a variation of the depth interview. A focus group interview is a discussion by a carefully selected group of representative consumers, opinion leaders, or experts. This group is usually made up of eight to twelve members. The participants are encouraged to express their own views on each topic or product and to elaborate on or react to the views of other group members. A specially trained group moderator will focus the group's discussion on a specific series of topics and/or products. The moderator usually follows a discussion guide designed to lead the discussion toward answering the research question or accomplishing specific study objectives.

The moderator starts with general questions. (Specifics are discussed after the respondents have freely exhausted the subject under discussion.) The questions are aimed at getting the respondents to express themselves—to reveal their opinions, experiences, and reactions.

Group sessions are generally tape-recorded or videotaped. The audio tapes are then listened to or transcribed and the results are analyzed. Focus group interviews are excellent sources of exploratory research.

Telephone Interviewing. Telephone interviewing is usually employed when the study design requires that the sample reflect a randomness of population (which would be too costly to do in person), when eligibility is difficult (requiring many contacts to obtain a completed interview), when the questionnaire is relatively short, or when face-to-face contact is not necessary. Telephone interviewing may be conducted either of the following two ways.

Interviewing may be conducted directly from the interviewer's home. The interviewers have all of the materials needed to complete an assignment in their homes and use the specified period on the telephone contacting respondents and conducting interviews.

In the second method, telephones may be installed in a room or in several rooms at a central location. They may be installed in a permanent office, in a hotel or motel, in a church basement, or, if a great many phones are required, in a ballroom. Central location interviewing has many advantages. It allows for constant monitoring and supervision. If an interviewer has a problem or question, it can be handled on the spot. Mistakes can be corrected, and respondents can be called back immediately if the supervisor finds that the interviewer's information is not complete. Interviews can be monitored to ensure that correct interviewing procedures, techniques, and quotas are being followed. Since telephone interviewing is the most commonly used method of data collection, a detailed discussion of the specific procedures of telephone interviewing is given in chapter 5.

Mail Interviewing. In mail surveying, some research is conducted by sending a self-addressed questionnaire to each potential respondent, along with a cover letter, completion instructions, a self-addressed stamped return envelope, and in some cases a token or incentive for the respondent to return the questionnaire. There is no personal interaction in most cases; however, sometimes a telephone call or personal contact is made to obtain agreement from the potential respondent before the questionnaire is mailed.

Advantages and Disadvantages of Communication Methods

Personal Communication. Personal interviews are the most productive, accurate, comprehensive, controlled, and versatile types of communication. There is ample opportunity for a well-trained interviewer to probe and interpret body language, facial expression, and other nuances during the interaction. Rapport can be developed to put the interviewee at ease and gain his or her cooperation. The interviewer can explain any misunderstanding the respondent might have and can keep the respondent on track and in sequence. In spite of the advantages of greater depth and productivity, the personal interview does take more time and money to administer.

Telephone Communication. Telephone interviews have the advantage of speed and relative economy compared to personal interviews. Phone interviews are also easily validated, and the personal interaction with a qualified interviewer maintains a relatively high degree of control. The proper sequencing of question and response can be maintained. While not as flexible and productive as a personal interview, a well-designed questionnaire administered over the phone by a skilled interviewer can gather relatively comprehensive information. The interviewer is also in a position to probe at appropriate times and to follow appropriate skip patterns. Weaknesses of the telephone interview include the inability to be very detailed because the respondent cannot be shown any products, pictures, or lists.

Mail Communication. Mail questionnaires allow for wide distribution. The lack of interviewer-respondent interaction can produce a feeling of anonymity that can encourage accurate responses to relatively sensitive questions. In theory, the respondent has time to check records or even confer with someone else to make sure that his or her information is accurate. The most positive use of mail questionnaires is with prerecruited consumer panels where respondents agree ahead of time to participate. In contrast to its advantages, there are several serious problems with this method of communication. Mail surveys generally have a low response rate, which results in nonresponse error. Control of the sample is minimal. It is impossible to know the difference in results between those who participated and those who did not. Too often the participants are either more interested in the subject area or have more free time to fill out questionnaires. In addition, a mail survey is slower, less flexible, and does not allow for probing. Control is lost with a mail questionnaire, sequencing is futile, and you never know who actually completed the questionnaire.

Procedures of
the Observation Method

Observation involves physically or mechanically recording some specific aspect of a consumer's activity or behavior. Some researchers contend that observation is more objective than communication. However, observation, whether in a field setting or in a laboratory, is not very versatile. Observation cannot answer questions concerning the attitudes, opinions, motivations, or intentions of consumers.

- Direct observation involves actually watching an individual's behavior. Purchase behavior is observed or the individual is viewed while actually using a specific product.
- Mechanical observation is sometimes appropriate. Various mechanical devices, such as cameras and counting instruments, are used to make observations. Eye motion, galvanic skin response, perspiration, pupil size, and various counting devices are examples of mechanical methods of measuring and recording activities.

SUMMARY OF PRIMARY DATA

Most research designs require the collection of both secondary and primary data. Primary data should be collected after exploratory results from a secondary data search are evaluated. This will allow the research to focus on collecting the specific relevant information needed to accomplish the research objectives effectively and efficiently.

chapter five

Designing the
Data-Gathering Instrument

Regardless of the type of survey method chosen, a questionnaire, survey guide, or other data-gathering instrument is required. Some research design specifications require a focus group interview that necessitates a generalized and open-ended study guide, while another research design methodology will call for a very detailed and structured questionnaire. The quality of the information gathered is directly proportional to the quality of the instrument designed to collect the data. Consequently, it is extremely important to construct the most effective data-gathering instrument possible.

As mentioned in chapter 3, it is vital to anticipate the total information needs of the project so that the data-gathering instrument can be designed to answer the research questions. The instrument must also gather the data in a form that will enable them to be subjected to the appropriate analysis techniques. The data-gathering instrument is the hinge that holds the research project together, and it must be well constructed.

THE QUESTIONNAIRE

A questionnaire is the main type of data-gathering instrument, even though discussion guides, recruiting qualifiers, screeners, and tally sheets are used from time to time. A questionnaire is defined in *Webster's New*

Collegiate Dictionary as "a set of questions for obtaining statistically useful or personal information from individuals." Obviously, an effective questionnaire is much more than that. A good questionnaire should accomplish the following purposes:

Purposes of a Questionnaire

1. *Express the study objectives in question form.* The questionnaire must capture the essence of the study objectives and ask questions whose answers will provide the information needed to answer the various research questions. Do not set study objectives adapted to an existing questionnaire that has been effective in the past. Each project, with its unique set of study objectives, should have a custom-made questionnaire designed especially for that project. The design of the questionnaire is the wrong place to try to economize.

2. *Measure the attitudes, behaviors, intentions, attributes, or other characteristics of the respondents.* The questions must be specific and reported in a form that will allow for comparisons to be made and results to be analyzed. The responses to the questions must provide the information necessary to answer the research questions in a format that can be subjected to the appropriate analytical technique. (Techniques of analysis will be discussed in chapter 8.)

3. *Strike a proper structural balance.* A questionnaire may be highly structured, with the exact wording specified and presented in exactly the same manner to each respondent, limiting the respondents to a predetermined set of answers. On the other hand, a questionnaire may be very unstructured, with all questions being open-ended and providing an opportunity for the interviewer to probe deeply. A "good" questionnaire is not necessarily a structured or unstructured one, but rather the questionnaire that has the right balance of structure to acquire accurate and appropriate information.

4. *Create harmony and rapport with the respondent.* A well-designed questionnaire targeted at the correct population sample should provide an enjoyable experience for the respondent. The frame of reference of the respondent must be considered in the design, wording, and sequencing of a questionnaire. Occupational jargon, cultural background, educational level, and regional differences can alter the effectiveness of a questionnaire. The questionnaire should appeal to the respondent, and it should also be designed so that the respondent can easily understand it, is able to answer it, and is willing to answer it.

5. *Provide just the right amount of information—no more, no less.* This statement is trite but true. There are often honest differences of opinion on just how much information is needed to answer a set of research questions. However, in designing a questionnaire the two basic

mistakes are (1) leaving an important question unasked, which makes the survey incomplete, and (2) asking too many irrelevant questions, which makes the survey unwieldy. A researcher must learn to economize in asking questions to avoid respondent "burnout," which leads to early terminations, incompleteness, and inaccurate information. Nonetheless, care must be taken in the design process to be ensured that the proper quantity of information is gathered to accomplish the research objectives.

Classifications of Questionnaires

Most questionnaires are classified in terms of their degree of *structure* and *disguise*. A structured questionnaire is one in which the questions and the possible range of responses are arranged in advance. The lack of deviation leads to a highly standardized instrument. An unstructured questionnaire is one in which questions are loosely predetermined and usually open-ended. This type of questionnaire allows the respondent great latitude in answering and affords the interviewer the opportunity to probe deeply into underlying aspects of the respondent's answers. Of course, there are questionnaires that fall all along the spectrum structure. Many questionnaires contain both highly structured portions and less structured portions.

When a questionnaire is classified according to disguise, it depends on how evident is the purpose of the question or questionnaire. An undisguised questionnaire is one in which the purpose of the research is obvious to the respondent because of the questions asked. A disguised questionnaire obscures the purpose of the research.

Based on the classification of a survey instrument according to structure and disguise, the following general types emerge:

1. *Structured-undisguised questionnaires*. These are the most commonly used questionnaires in research today. Every respondent is posed the same questions in the same sequence, with the same range of possible responses. In most cases the purpose of the research is clearly stated in an introductory statement or is obvious from the questions asked. This type of instrument has the adantages of simplicity in administration, tabulation, and analysis; standardized data collection; objectivity; and reliability. The disadvantages include less opportunity for probing and less validity. This type is most effective when the range of possible responses is narrow. For example, it is appropriate for obtaining data on attitudes, intentions, opinions, and demographic, psychographic, and socioeconomic characteristics.

2. *Structured-disguised questionnaires*. These are probably the least often used questionnaires in market research. They maintain the advantages of structuring while attempting to add the advantage of disguise in eliminating possible bias from the respondents' knowledge of the purpose

of the survey. The main advantages are ease of administration, coding, tabulating, and analysis.

3. *Unstructured-undisguised questionnaires*. In this type of questionnaire the respondent is usually aware of the purpose of the survey, but the responses are not restricted. Freedom is allowed for the interviewer to probe and for the respondent to express deeper views and opinions. This type of questionnaire is appropriate for depth interviews and focus group interviews. It allows the interviewer or moderator the privilege of beginning with a general question or series of questions and allowing the discussion to develop following a general series of questions or a discussion guide. With this type of questionnaire, the effectiveness of the depth or focus group interview depends largely upon the skills of the interviewer or moderator. Advantages of the method are that more in-depth and accurate responses can be obtained, particularly for complex and sensitive issues, and greater cooperation and involvement can be obtained from the respondent. The disadvantages lie in the fact that so much depends on the interviewer. Bias can come into play. The unstructured nature of the data causes problems with accurate analysis. The high cost involved in administering this type of questionnaire is also a disadvantage. The unstructured-undisguised interview is well suited for exploratory research, gaining background, and generating and clarifying research questions.

4. *Unstructured-disguised questionnaires*. This type of questionnaire is appropriate for depth interviews and focus group interviews when circumstances dictate that the purpose of the survey be kept from the respondents for fear that such knowledge will seriously bias the results. In some depth interviews, the first portion follows an unstructured-disguised format while the second portion shifts to an unstructured-undisguised approach with the introduction of the purpose, a product, or another concept involved in the research. The advantages and disadvantages of loose structure and disguise hold true for this type of questionnaire. Unstructured-disguised questionnaires are often used in motivation research to determine the "why's" of an individual's behavior.

STEPS IN
DESIGNING A QUESTIONNAIRE

There is no precise methodology for the step-by-step design of a questionnaire. Various research texts have suggested procedures ranging from four to fourteen sequential steps. Questionnaire design, no matter how formalized, still requires a measure of science and a measure of art, with a good dose of humility mixed in. In designing a questionnaire, presumption must be set aside. Although for simplicity of format the sequence for developing a questionnaire is given here in a step-by-step manner, rarely is a questionnaire actually constructed in such a routine way. Quite often it is necessary to skip from one step to another and to loop back through a previous series of steps.

The following steps represent a sequential procedure that must be considered for the development of an effective survey instrument.

1. Determine the specific information needed to answer the research questions.
2. Identify the sources of the required information.
3. Choose the type of questionnaire and the method of administration that suits the information required and the sources of information.
4. Determine the types of questions to be used and the form of the responses.
5. Develop the specific questions to be asked.
6. Determine the sequence of the questions and the length of the questionnaire.
7. Predetermine coding and measurement methodology.
8. Pretest the questionnaire.
9. Review and revise the questionnaire.

Determining the Specific Information Needed

The initial step in the design of a questionnaire is to determine the specific information needed to answer the research questions. This task is made much easier if the earliest phases of the research process have been accomplished precisely. Clear study objectives facilitate this important decision. One of the most common and costly errors of research is the omission of an important question on the data-gathering instrument. Once the questionnaire is fielded, it is too late to go back for additional information without significant delay and additional cost. Consequently, the researcher must determine all of the information required before the questionnaire is developed. All efforts must be marshalled at this point to ensure relevant results for the analysis phase of the research process. In some cases it is advisable to conduct exploratory research so that all of the relevant variables are identified. Focus groups, reviews of secondary sources of information, and some selected personal interviews are good ways of making sure that the pertinent variables are identified.

Identifying the Sources

Step 2 involves the important aspect of identifying the sources of the information requirements determined in step 1. Sample selection will be discussed in more detail in chapter 7; however, the characteristics of the sample frame are extremely important in designing the data-gathering instrument. The sophistication, intelligence, frame of reference, location, ethnic background, and other characteristics of the potential respondents are vital in determining the type of questionnaire, the wording of the questions, the means of administration, and other aspects of the questionnaire.

Choosing the Type of Questionnaire and the Method of Administration

Step 3 involves utilizing the results of steps 1 and 2 to decide whether a structured or unstructured, disguised or undisguised questionnaire is most appropriate. The decision must also be made about whether a personal interview, telephone survey, or mail questionnaire is most acceptable. These decisions should be made with regard to the information required and the nature of the information sources. Other considerations that affect this decision are the cost and time constraints placed on the research project. (The cost and time advantages of the methods of administration were discussed in chapter 4.)

Determining the Types of Questions

Step 4 is to choose the types of questions to be used in the questionnaire. To accomplish this the researcher must look both backward and forward. The researcher looks backward to review the information required and the nature of the respondents. This can dictate various decisions concerning the types of questions selected. The researcher must also look forward to the analysis stage of the research process to ensure that the right levels of measurement are obtained to accommodate the correct analysis methodology.

There are five basic types of questions that might be used in a questionnaire. Most questionnaires have more than one type of question.

1. *Open-ended questions*. Open-ended questions impose no limit on the range of replies the respondent can make. This type of question is useful if you don't know what the possible replies might be, when you want to have verbatim responses, and when you want to gain deep insight into attitudes on sensitive issues. Open-ended questions are also helpful in breaking the ice with the respondent and providing background information for more detailed questions. The weaknesses of this type of question are that they are hard to word and ask naturally, all words cannot be recorded (which introduces an element of bias), they are biased favorably toward more literate respondents, and they provide qualitative instead of quantitative data.

2. *Dichotomous questions*. A question that gives two choices, either

"yes" or "no" or a choice of two opposite alternatives, is called a dichoto-mous question. These questions are useful for starting an interview, are easy to tabulate, and can be used as a lead-in for more specific questions to a particular group. A weakness of dichotomous questions is that they can force a choice where none exists (like the classic, "Do you still beat your wife?"). Another weakness is that few questions can be framed in terms of a dichotomy.

3. *Multiple-choice questions.* Multiple-choice questions provide sev-eral alternatives. In some cases the respondent may be asked to select only one answer from a list or to select as many responses as are appli-cable. The advantages of the multiple-choice question are ease of admin-istration, ease of tabulation, and flexibility for factual as well as attitudinal responses. Some disadvantages arise from the length of the list of alterna-tive responses, the fact that the list is not exhaustive, and the fact that reading the list may lead the respondent.

4. *Scales.* Although a scale can be considered a multiple-choice ques-tion, it deserves separate consideration. Scales are used to measure degrees of feelings, attitudes, interest, and intentions. A respondent is asked to place his or her opinion on a scale from one end of a spectrum to another. Quite often the range will be from "poor" to "excellent," "very satisfied" to "very dissatisfied," "very important" to "not important at all," "very interested" to "not at all interested." The scale is often on a five-, seven-, or ten-point range. The benefit of a scale is that it permits the objective measurement of attitudes and feelings. This allows for the identification of segments of respondents who are more favorably inclined toward a product, service, or issue. Scaling is somewhat subject to various frame-of-reference differences and to the halo effect.

5. *Projective questions.* In some research circumstances indirect approaches to data gathering are preferred. The Rorschach ink-blot test is an example of an indirect projective technique. Other methods of this type are word association, sentence completion, and storytelling. The respondent is given much latitude in interpreting the questions.

Developing the Specific Questions

Step 5 in the construction of a questionnaire is to actually write the specific questions to be asked. The completion of the first four steps will, to a large extent, control the content of the questions. The wording should be as understandable and explicit as possible. Questions should be worded so that leading, pressuring, or embarrassing the respondent are avoided. Ambiguous words with vague meanings should also be shunned. Basic rules for wording questions are:

1. Keep the questions short, simple, and to the point.

2. Avoid identifying the sponsor of the survey.

3. Keep the questions as neutral as possible.

4. Don't ask unnecessary questions.

5. Avoid asking questions that the respondent either cannot or will not answer.

6. Keep the tone of the questions positive.

7. Avoid asking leading or overly personal questions.

Determining Sequence and Length of the Questionnaire

Step 6 can be extremely important in the completion rate of the survey. Excessive length may deter a number of respondents from completing the survey. This step can be equally important to the quality of the results obtained. The sequence of the questions should follow a logical pattern and flow smoothly and effortlessly from one section to another. Another important consideration is to ensure that questions that build on previous questions are placed correctly in the questionnaire.

Most questionnaires have three basic sections:

1. *Introduction*. The introduction tells the respondent who the researcher is, why the respondent's information is being requested, and what is expected of the respondent. The introduction should explain the purpose of the questionnaire and enlist the cooperation of the respondent. In the case of a mail survey this may take place in an attached cover letter. On the phone this is accomplished by using a positive tone without sounding like a polished sales pitch. Most people want to express their opinions as long as they know the survey is not a sales gimmick. The introduction should promise to keep the respondent's identity and information confidential. The introduction may qualify the respondent in a special way to make sure that the interviewer is talking only to the right respondents.

2. *Body or content*. The body or main content of the questionnaire provides the basic information required by the research objectives. This is usually the most substantial portion of the questionnaire. If the respondent has not been qualified in the introduction, the first question of this section should identify the proper respondents and give instructions to end the survey for all others. This section should start out with easy, direct questions, leaving personal or sensitive questions until the end. Once respondents have become interested in the survey, they are more likely to respond to personal or sensitive issues.

3. *Classification*. The final section of most questionnaires is designed to obtain cross-classification information, such as sex, income, educational level, occupation, marital status, and age. These demographic data allow

for comparisons among different types of respondents. Certain market segments may emerge through the use of this cross-classification data.

Predetermining Coding and Levels of Measurement Methodology

Step 7 emphasizes the importance of good feedback from the respondent back to the interviewer. A successful project not only needs clear and accurate information, but it also requires data that can be measured meaningfully. Most surveys generate both qualitative and quantitative data. The quantitative data can be analyzed readily. Some of the most important responses, particularly those related to attitudes and opinions, are often the results of open-ended questions and are difficult to categorize. Unless the results can be grouped, there can be no significant comparison of these results. The judicious use of scales can translate what would ordinarily be qualitative information into a quantifiable form. The scaling technique is an attempt to establish a direct measure of a respondent's attitude or opinion.

There are four basic levels of numerical data. Nominal and ordinal scales are lower forms of measurement, while interval and ratio scales produce data that support stronger quantitative analysis.

1. *Nominal scale.* A nominal scale is established by using numbers to identify or categorize things. I.D. numbers of a sort, zip codes, and telephone numbers are good examples of this type of scale. The numbers simply identify. They are assigned on an arbitrary basis. One number is not superior to another. Consequently, means and medians and any statistical technique that depends on them are meaningless.

2. *Ordinal scale.* An ordinal scale is developed when items are ordered with no regard to the interval between the ranks. This scale simply determines order. Each object is ranked in accordance to some attribute. For example, an ordinal scale will state that one person is taller than another person, but not how much taller. The data can be ranked, but an evaluation of the differences cannot be made.

3. *Interval scale.* An interval scale also orders items by rank; however, in this case actual values are given to the items with equal distance between any pair of adjacent items. An interval scale also features an arbitrary zero point. This allows for comparisons of differences. The classical example of this type of scale is the thermometer. Means and standard deviations can be computed from interval scales.

4. *Ratio scale.* A ratio scale is an interval scale that has a natural zero point. Because of this the ratio between any two points on the scale can be measured. This allows for a comparison of absolute magnitude. Weight, length, and units sold are examples of this type of scale. Most methods of statistical analysis can be performed on this type of data.

Pretesting the Questionnaire

The eighth step is essential and should not be ignored. A questionnaire should never be administered until it has been pretested. A questionnaire may be too long, ambiguous, incomplete, unclear, or biased in some way. Not only will a thorough pretest help overcome these problems, but a pretest will help refine any procedural problems the questionnaire might have, such as improper skip patterns and misunderstanding the interviewer. A pretest will evaluate and fine-tune the questionnaire, estimate the time required for completion of the interview, check for problems with ambiguous questions or unanticipated responses, and allow for a setup of coding refinements for tabulations. The pretest should be administered under actual field conditions in order to get an accurate response. If significant changes result from an original pretest, it is advisable to conduct a second pretest after appropriate revisions have been made. A relatively small number of interviews is sufficient to pretest a normal questionnaire. Once these have been completed, all interviewers who participated should report their findings. They will then be able to determine whether the questions work and make suggestions for revision.

Revising the Questionnaire

Based on the pretest and a thorough review of all the preceding steps, the questionnaire should finally be revised. The bottom line for an effective data-gathering instrument is the accuracy of the data collected. Everything that can possibly be done in advance should be done to ensure the accuracy of the instrument.

SUMMARY

No matter what type of survey method is used, a data-gathering instrument is generally required to gather the data required to answer the research questions. Good data-gathering instruments should reflect the research needs by reiterating the study objectives in question form; they should accurately measure attitudes, behaviors, intentions, attributes, and other characteristics of respondents; they should be concise and balanced in structure; and they should create harmony and rapport with the respondents. A questionnaire should provide just the right amount of information—no more, no less.

The steps to be followed in designing a data-gathering instrument are determining the specific information required to answer the research questions, identifying the sources of the required information, choosing the type of questionnaire and the method of administration that suits the information required and the sources of information, determining the types of questions to be used and the form of the responses, developing the specific questions to be asked, determining the sequence of the questions and the length of the questionnaire, predetermining coding and measurement methodology, pretesting the instrument, and reviewing, revising, and pretesting again if necessary.

chapter six

Fielding the Data-Gathering Instrument

Once all steps are accomplished in the preparation of a questionnaire, it is ready for the field. The field operation phase of the research process begins when the data collection instrument is taken to the source of the information. The planning of the field work is closely related to the preparation of the questionnaire, which was discussed in chapter 5, and the sample selection, which will be discussed in chapter 7. All three of these aspects of data gathering must be well conceived, planned, and executed in order to achieve the objectives of a study. Error can occur in all of these phases, and the field collection portion is no exception. The results of any excellently conceived questionnaire drawn from a scientifically selected, representative sample can be nullified by errors in the fielding of the questionnaire.

PLANNING

To minimize error and to gather accurate information as efficiently as possible, the field service of a questionnaire should be well planned. Time, money, and personnel must all be budgeted. Time for the field portion is extremely important, since it must fit into the overall time frame of the entire project. The field service should have a realistic completion date with a little leeway. This will allow for timely and accurate completion. Since the field work must be done before analysis can occur, good sequencing is necessary.

BUDGETING

Money must be budgeted appropriately for the field service effort. Cost must be assigned to all of the component activities of the field service phase. Cost estimates must be made for wages of interviewers, supervisors, and general office support; telephone charges; postage; production of the questionnaire and other forms; and supplies.

STAFFING

Personnel is the key to successful field service operations. Care must be taken to have the best possible personnel to accomplish the research task. There is no substitute for well-trained, experienced interviewers. Consequently, the personnel must not only be selected and scheduled for a project, but they must also have been trained in the techniques of interviewing. Some of the basic rules of interviewing are discussed later in this chapter. Another important part of preparing the personnel for a specific study is to ensure that they are thoroughly briefed on the specific aspects of the questionnaire that will be administered. The personnel must have a clear understanding of the instrument and what information is desired.

GUIDELINES
FOR INTERVIEWERS

The field service operation should accomplish the following responsibilities:

1. Cover the sample frame in accordance with instructions to ensure representative data. The proper areas and individuals must be contacted.
2. Follow study procedures and administer the questionnaire as written. Be familiar with the questionnaire before beginning.
3. Write down responses verbatim. Record all other responses according to instructions in the proper terms of measurement.
4. Probe, but do not lead. If a person does not understand the question, read it again verbatim, perhaps more slowly or with more inflection.
5. Establish rapport with the interviewee. Be confident in what you are doing

and assume that people will talk to you. Most people love to have the opportunity to say what they think. Reflect enthusiasm for what you are doing.

6. Accomplish a field edit to ensure that the data are being collected in appropriate form.

PERSONAL INTERVIEWS

The requirement of personal interviews creates special problems from the field service point of view. Interviewers must be located, screened, hired, trained, briefed, and sent out in the proper geographic areas called for in the sampling plan. A company will often hire outside field service organizations to conduct this type of interviewing. If a company has subcontracted the entire project to an outside consultant firm, it would be wise to make sure that the research firm has its own in-house field service personnel or at least has a good network of field services to which it subcontracts. Interviewers must also be well trained in the art of interviewing, but quite often they must also understand technical terms and jargon, particularly in industrial marketing research. This high degree of competence and preparation on the part of interviewers, along with the time and travel involved, makes this form of interviewing quite expensive.

TELEPHONE INTERVIEWS

Some of the same considerations involved with the development and management of personal interviewers also apply to telephone interviewers. However, greater control of a telephone interviewing staff can be maintained, particularly if the work is accomplished from a central telephone location. The entire interviewing effort can be monitored by a trained supervisor. On-the-spot questions can be answered and field editing can be accomplished to allow for quick correction of any problems with the instrument. WATS, MCI, Sprint, U.S. Telephone, and other lower-than-normal rate systems can be used to appreciably lower long-distance charges.

Currently, telephone interviewing is the most widely utilized type of survey communication. This is true because of the time and financial advantages of the method. Callbacks can be made much more easily, and many people will talk on the phone when they would not open their door to talk with a stranger.

MAIL INTERVIEWS

Mail interviews eliminate the problems of selecting, training, and supervising interviewers; however, they create some of their own problems such as lack of response and coverage, inability to control the sample responding, time lags in response, and potential for misinterpretation of questions.

The procedures for mail surveys is the same as for questionnaire development: pretesting, finalization, and production. However, the mail survey eliminates the field service worker. In place of the personal or telephone interview there is a mailing or series of mailings. Postcard reminders, incentives, tokens, and follow-up questionnaires may be sent at appropriate times to encourage return of questionnaires.

THE INTERVIEWING RELATIONSHIP

The first step in the interviewing process requires the interviewer to obtain the cooperation of the potential respondent and then to develop rapport with the respondent to allow the interviewer to obtain the needed information. If the interview is on an informal, conversational basis, the respondent will be at ease and will not hesitate to voice his or her real opinions. To be conversational and informal, an interviewer need not lose control of the situation. A balance should be sought between the stiff, formal inquisition, in which questions are grimly read off and answers methodically checked, and the situation where the interviewer is too friendly and is out of control. An interview in which twenty minutes are spent on the actual questions and twenty minutes more are devoted to irrelevancies and conversation is inefficient.

Rapport

Rapport is the term used to describe the personal relationship of confidence and understanding between the interviewer and the respondent; rapport provides the foundation for good interviewing. A prerequisite to good rapport is that the respondent should know where he or she stands in the interview. The interview is actually a new situation for most people and, when it begins, the respondent does not know what is expected or how far he or she can safely go in expressing opinions. Obviously, a respondent will react more favorably and openly in a situation he or she understands and accepts. The respondent should understand that the interview is confidential and important, that the interviewer is a friendly person who is ready to listen, and that he or she can discuss the interview topics in detail. Throughout the interview, and especially in its early stages, the interviewer makes a careful effort to establish the tone of the interview in the respondent's mind. The respondent comes to have a clear idea of where he or she stands and what roles he or she and the interviewer have. The respondent should be made to understand that there are no right or wrong answers, that the interviewer is only interested in his unbiased responses to a question. Most people like to share their opinions. Good rapport, coupled with a well designed data gathering instrument, should serve the goal of making the interview a very positive experience for the respondent.

THE INTERVIEWING SITUATION

• The approach an interviewer takes is extremely important. In order for the sample to be representative, it is important that potential respondents are not "lost" or passed by because of something an interviewer may do to cause the potential respondent to refuse to participate or be excluded from the sample.

The method of approach will vary a great deal according to circumstances. As a general rule, the following approach works well:

"Hello. I'm   (Name)   from   (Agency) . We're conducting a survey in this area on   (Subject) , and I'd like   (your)   opinion."

Notice the introduction does not ask, "May I ask you some questions?"; "Are you busy?"; "Would you mind answering some questions?"; or "Could you spare a couple of minutes?" These are approaches that allow the respondent to say "No" easily and should be avoided.

• The interviewer should make sure that the respondent qualifies for the survey. If only certain types of people are specified for in the study, no compromise can be made. In all surveys, only one member per household may be interviewed. Including more than one interview per household will bias the survey.

• The respondent should not be misled about how long an interview might take. In long interviews it is helpful to state the time required before the interview begins. However, the interviewer need not call attention to time or to the length of the interview unless the respondent asks or appears to be in a hurry.

• Should a respondent initially decline to be interviewed, the interviewer should not give up too easily. He or she should be patient, calm, and pleasantly conversational. Often, a potential respondent who has initially refused will then agree to participate. If a person is completely opposed to being interviewed, the interviewer should go on to find another respondent. In some cases the selected respondent is actually too busy or is getting ready to go out, so that an interview at that time is impossible. The interviewer should give a general introduction and try to stimulate the respondent's interest to the extent that he or she will be willing to be interviewed at a later time. The interviewer may need to suggest several alternative times before a convenient time is agreed upon for the interview.

Respondents may ask why they were selected. The interviewer should explain that they were selected at random as one of a very few people in the area to take part in the survey. The respondent should be told that there are no right or wrong answers; the interviewer is only interested in candid opinions. The respondent should be told that his or her responses are confidential and that his or her identity will not be disclosed since the responses will be grouped or tabulated along with hundreds of other interviews.

• If at all possible, the respondent should be interviewed alone. The presence of other people may influence the respondent's answers. From time to time the respondent may be accompanied by a friend who may begin to answer the questions with or for the respondent. The interviewer should remind them that he or she is interested only in the opinions of the respondent. In such a situation, if the friend is not a member of the same household as the respondent, another interviewer may interview the friend.

• The interviewer should be completely familiar with the questionnaire and all survey materials before conducting an interview. Practice interviews should be conducted to ensure that the interviewer will not be clumsy with his or her first respondents.

• The interviewer should know and follow the instructions that are actually printed in capital letters or enclosed in parentheses. They will indicate:

1. Skip patterns (telling which questions to ask when a specific answer is given).
2. When to read or not read possible answers.
3. When only one answer may be recorded or when multiple answers are acceptable.

• Legibility is of paramount importance in filling out the questionnaire. A lot of time may be wasted in the tabulation process by trying to decipher what was written. The interviewer should always take time at the end of the interview to scan the work and rewrite any words that may be difficult for someone else to read. Each interview should be checked to see that it is entirely legible and understandable. The interviewer should always use a lead pencil with sufficiently dark lead. Do not use colored pencils or any form of ink; a number 2 lead pencil is preferable.

• Each question on a questionnaire has been designed for a specific purpose to obtain the information required to accomplish the study objectives. If an interviewer were to record or put the questions into his or her own words, this would introduce a bias and his or her interviews would no longer be like those of other interviewers who are asking the questions as stated on the questionnaire.

In the case where a respondent does not seem to understand the question, the interviewer should repeat the question slowly, but without explaining it in his or her own words. If the respondent cannot answer or refuses to answer a question, the circumstances should be noted in the margin and the interviewer should go on to the next question.

• The interviewer must not lead the respondent; he or she should not ask anything that would direct the respondent to give an answer that he or she thinks the interviewer wants. The interviewer should never suggest a word, phrasing, or idea to the respondent. An example of leading would be as follows:

> *Respondent:* "It tasted good."
>
> *Interviewer:* "By good, do you mean fresh?"
>
> *Respondent:* "Yes."

• It is human nature to ask a question in a negative way. Instead of asking, "What else do you remember?" the interviewer may ask, "Don't you remember anything else?" or "Can't you remember anything else?" By asking a question in a negative way, the interviewer may put the respondent on the defensive, and continued negative questioning may lead to irritation and termination of the interview. Furthermore, the normal reply to a negative probe is a negative response.

• Not only should the question be asked verbatim but the interviewer should also record the answers verbatim. The interviewer will usually be able to keep up with the respondent. If the answer rushes on, the interviewer may have to repeat each of the respondent's words as he or she writes. The respondent usually slows down when this is done. Or, the interviewer may have to say, "You were saying something about. . ." The respondent will usually go back and cover the point again.

Another way to slow down the respondent is to say that his or her answer is very important and the interviewer wants to be sure to get every word down.

The exact words of the respondent capture more of the flavor of the response through the use of pet phrases and words. The interviewer must record the answers in the respondent's exact words. The interviewer must not edit or rephrase the respondent's answer. Responses are recorded in the first person exactly as the respondent states them.

• Unless otherwise specified by survey instructions, closed-ended responses should be noted with an "X," which has proven to be more legible than a checkmark.

If the instructions indicate that the interviewer is to circle a specified number of the questionnaire to indicate a respondent's answer, it should be neatly circled and the circle should not extend around a second word or number. When a grid format is used for responses, care should be taken to circle the answer in the column number corresponding to the question number.

• The interviewer must remain completely neutral. A respondent's answers can very easily be biased if the interviewer interjects voice inflections, biased comments, or facial gestures.

The respondent should not be rushed. Some people just do not think or converse as rapidly as others. It should be recognized that the respondent is being asked for an opinion without prior preparation and about which he or she has had very little time to think.

The interviewer does not have to have an expressionless face. He or she should develop the habit of encouraging the respondent to talk, without leading, and then listen carefully to what is said. There are many ways to indicate that the interviewer is following the respondent's remarks. Sometimes a nod of the head is sufficient; sometimes unbiased remarks like "I see what you mean," "I understand," or "That's interesting," will keep the respondent expressing ideas and thinking further about the topic without leading or biasing the data.

• After completing the interview, the respondent should be thanked. Before the interviewer leaves, he or she should review the responses to all questions to be certain that they have been answered correctly and that the answers are clear, meaningful, and legible. The interviewer should then leave as quickly and courteously as possible.

• Generally, questionnaires include some classification questions such as income, age, educational level, occupation, and other demographic or statistical information. Most people answer such questions willingly. Refusals will be rare if these questions are asked properly in an unapologetic fashion. Respondents may also be told that the answers are tabulated by a computer and that no one answer will be looked at individually.

• The interviewer must be careful to record legibly the respondent's identifying information so that there can be no mistake in contacting the designated respondent for purposes of validation. About 10 to 15 percent of all interviews will be verified. If the respondent refuses to give his or her full name, a first name is sufficient.

GENERAL RULES OF INTERVIEWING

1. *Security of the Survey.* The questionnaires, the responses, and all materials used in conjunction with the survey are confidential and should be returned to the supervisor at the completion of the interviewing.

Respondents must never be told who is the sponsor of the study. The interviewer should not discuss the survey with family, friends, other interviewers, or anyone else. Confidentiality of the client is of utmost importance.

2. *Briefings*. Briefings, or training sessions, will be held before each project. The entire job will be discussed, giving both the supervisor and the interviewers an opportunity to carefully study job specifications and instructions and to ask any questions pertaining to the job. Practice interviews will also be conducted to familiarize interviewers with the questionnaire. Individuals will be assigned quotas or specific duties involved with the job.

3. *Supervisor Assistance*. If a question or problem arises, the interviewer should ask the job supervisor, not another interviewer, for assistance. Once called to the supervisor's attention, any questions or problems can be remedied for all interviewers on the job or can be referred to the client.

4. *Not Interviewing Friends or Acquaintances*. A friend or acquaintance of the interviewer might answer the questions in a manner that he or she thinks will please the interviewer instead of giving a candid response.

5. *Adherence to Study Specifications*. The specifications of a study have been set forth for very definite reasons, and the specifications must be followed, to the letter. Therefore, if the interviewing method is personal, the interviewer cannot interview a respondent on the telephone; if the interviewer is to contact only one person in the household, he or she cannot interview other family members; if the interviewer is to interview one person at a time, he or she cannot interview a group of respondents. The interviewer cannot interview the same respondent for multiple studies at the same interview. If he or she did any of these things, the interviewer would not be following the specifications and the interviews would be rendered useless.

6. *Following Study Procedures and Instructions*. It is very important for each interview to be conducted in the same manner by all interviewers. Instructions about showing exhibit cards, posters, or keeping products concealed must be obeyed the same way in all interviews. All study procedures and instructions must be followed.

7. *Accurate Record Keeping*. It is the interviewer's responsibility to keep accurate records of all information required by the supervisor or the client. If the addition of columns of numbers is required, the correctness of the addition is the interviewer's responsibility. Information collected through the use of a tally sheet is often just as important as information collected in the actual interview.

8. *Completing Assignments on Time*. An interviewer assumes the responsibility for completing an assignment within the specified time

period. Should unforeseen circumstances prevent completion of an assignment, the interviewer should notify his or her supervisor immediately. In addition, the supervisor should be notified immediately if the interviewer anticipates that he or she will not complete the assignment within the specified time.

9. *Work Efficiency.* Two factors affecting the efficiency of work performance are speed and quality. Conducting interviews at a reasonable speed is important. However, quality should never be sacrificed to speed for the sake of numbers. On the other hand, gaining desired information from the respondent is critical and can be done without spending undue time on any one area.

10. *Probing.* Many questions in in-depth interviews are open-ended and require the interviewer to coax the answers from the respondent. Getting as much information as possible from open-ended questions often requires skillful probing. The interviewer should never assume anything about what the respondent is implying, but he or she should probe to get clear and complete answers to all parts of the question in the respondent's own words. The two basic purposes of probing are (1) to clarify, and (2) to develop additional information.

• *Clarity.* The interviewer should get as much information as possible from open-ended questions. An answer that tells something specific is much more valuable than getting several answers that are vague. The interviewer's objective should be to clarify why the respondent gave a particular answer to one of the questions. The more concrete and specific these reasons are, the more valuable the information becomes. For example, a respondent is talking about a car that he believes would be economical. What does he mean by "economical"? He could mean that it's not very expensive to buy, that it gets good gas mileage, that it's not very expensive to maintain, that it has a high trade-in value, or something else. It's up to the interviewer to find out precisely what he means by "economical."

Here is an example of how to probe for clarity:

Respondent: "It's not my kind of movie."

Interviewer: "Why do you say that?"

Respondent: "It doesn't look interesting."

Interviewer: "What do you mean by interesting"?

Respondent: "The thread of the picture seems difficult to follow; the action is slow and drawn out. I enjoy fast-paced, action-packed movies."

• *Developing Additional Information.* An interviewer must often get respondents to expand on an answer. "It would be true to life," or "It makes you think," and other general answers should be probed by saying,

"Why do you say that?" or, "Tell me more about that." Many of the best probes are on key words, and the interviewer may repeat the key words from the respondent's answer on a question: "True to life?" or "Makes you think?"

Here is an example of probing for additional information:

Respondent: "They showed a bowl of soup."

Interviewer: "What kind of soup was it?"

Respondent: "It looked like vegetable soup."

Interviewer: "What else did they show?"

Respondent: "A little boy eating the soup and smiling because he liked it."

Interviewer: "What did they say about the soup?"

Respondent: "They said this soup makes a warm and nutritious meal in itself."

Technical Aspects of Probing

1. When a key word in a respondent's answer is being probed, it should be underlined: "I thought the soup looked tasty."
2. Probing questions that are not tied to key words should be indicated by prefacing them with a (P).
3. Answers should always be recorded verbatim in the respondent's own words. The interviewer should not edit, try to improve the grammar, or put things in complete sentences. Abbreviations may be used as long as they are obvious to anyone who might see them. If they are not, go back after the interview and write them out.
4. The interviewer should begin writing the minute the respondent begins to speak.
5. If necessary, the interviewer may ask the respondent to stop for a minute or to repeat something he or she missed.
6. The interviewer should never lead the respondent. Legitimate probes must be distinguished from leading questions, such as "Was it a bowl of vegetable soup?" or "Do you remember the little boy in the ad?" Anything that suggests something about the subject is inadmissible.

Probing Summary

1. Get specifics.
2. Ask "What else?" only after probing the original response.
3. Do not just accept an adjective or a thought—*find out why* the respondent feels that way.
4. Get the respondents to expand on their answers.
5. Details about the subject, whether positive or negative, are very important.

ERRORS IN DATA COLLECTION

The accuracy of any data provided in a research project depends on several interrelated things. First, there must have been clearly articulated research objectives. Second, correct design must have been accomplished. Third, correct sampling techniques and procedures must have been used. Fourth, the data must have been collected well. Finally, the data must be analyzed correctly. Mistakes or errors at any point can negate excellent design, sampling technique, questionnaire design, and so on.

Many types of errors are generally classified as sampling and nonsampling errors. A *sampling error* is the difference between the observed values of a specific variable and the average of a series of observed values over a period of time. This is a statistical error resulting from the fact that any given sample has an opportunity to produce a different estimate of the parameter than is actually the case. *Nonsampling errors* commonly arise from errors in design, logic, interpretation, field service, or presentation. Nonsampling field errors are discussed below, while sampling errors are discussed in chapter 7.

Errors of the nonsampling variety are a numerous breed. They are pervasive in nature and are highly arbitrary. Unlike sampling errors, nonsampling errors do not necessarily decrease with sample size. They may, in fact, increase. While sampling errors can be estimated, the direction, magnitude, and impact of nonsampling errors are generally unknown. As a result, nonsampling errors are frequently the most significant errors that arise during a research project. Their reduction is not dependent on increasing sample size, but on improving methods and procedures for handling the data themselves.

Types of Nonsampling Errors

There are two basic types of nonsampling errors: nonobservational error and observational error. *Nonobservational error* relates to the fact that certain parts of the survey population did not provide data for the study. This could result if part of the population of interest was not included or because some of the population did not respond. *Observational errors* occur because the information gathered is inaccurate or because mistakes are made while the data are being processed. Quite often, observational errors are made without the researcher being aware of them. This makes them potentially dangerous to the outcome of the project.

Nonobservational errors generally consist of noncoverage and nonresponse errors.

Noncoverage Errors.. These occur when some elements of the original population are not included in the sample. The bias from this type of error is the difference in characteristics, attributes, and opinions between those who respond and those who do not. This is a very troublesome problem in marketing research because it is not known if there are significant and strategic differences between the ones who did not respond and the ones who did when there is no information on the nonrespondents. Noncoverage is basically a problem with the sampling frame. The sampling frame is a listing of all possible members of the population being studied. All of the basic survey methods depend on such a listing. Telephone directories are not complete frames of a city's population. Not every household has a telephone. Of those that do, many have unlisted numbers and many people are in transition at any given time. Mail surveys have the same noncoverage problems, because it is rare to find a list that includes exactly the total population under study.

In many cases noncoverage of certain portions of the sample frame leads to overcoverage of other portions. Overcoverage can also occur when certain sample units are listed more than once. This leads to double counting and study bias.

As important as the noncoverage that results from not including all possible respondents in the sample frame is the noncoverage of sample members. This occurs when the listed sample units are not contacted. This occurs in both personal and telephone surveys. Quite often, this happens when interviewers do not follow instructions or do not make the appropriate callbacks.

The most effective way to limit the extent of noncoverage error is to recognize its existence and take correctional measures. These measures are (1) to improve the sample frame, (2) to establish clear instructions concerning whom to interview, when to interview, and where to interview, (3) to specify callback requirements, and (4) when possible, to verify or monitor interviews.

Nonresponse Errors. These errors occur when some of the elements of the population selected to be part of the sample do not respond. This happens most frequently with mail surveys, but it can also occur in telephone surveys and personal interviews. The people originally chosen to be interviewed might not respond because they are not at home or because they refuse to participate.

The "not at home" category is on the increase. Included here are the respondents who are literally not at home and those who cannot be located. This includes those who are out for the day, gone on an extended trip, or even those who have recently moved. There is some evidence that the "not at home" categories of respondents tend to have different characteristics than those who are more easily located. The "not at homes" tend to be younger, better educated, more affluent, and more urban than those who are "at home." Dual-career households tend to aggravate the problem. Care must be taken to account for the "not at home" factor, or survey results will be incomplete and biased. The segments less likely to be home will be underrepresented, and the results will be skewed toward the more commonly "at home" respondents.

Some respondents may refuse to participate or may terminate prematurely after beginning the survey. The actual rate of refusal will depend on the nature of the respondent, the subject of the research, the ability of the interviewer, the length and design of the questionnaire, and the

personal situation of the respondent. Mail surveys are particularly suscep-
tible to the refusal nonresponse error. Personal and telephone interviews
are also plagued with refusal nonresponse. Overall, the refusal rate
appears to be increasing. More and more people are being interviewed,
and the novelty of being surveyed is wearing off. Because of fraud and
crime, people are hesitant to allow interviewers into their homes. The
use of the phone for sales pitches disguised as surveys has also made
legitimate surveys more difficult to complete.

Fortunately, there are many effective methods of reducing nonresponse problems. Some of the most common ones are:

1. Sell the respondent on the importance of his or her opinion and the value
   of the research.
2. Notify the respondent in advance and make an appointment for a callback
   at a mutually agreeable time.
3. Assure the respondent of confidentiality.
4. Follow up with a callback or a follow-up mailing.
5. Include return postage and envelopes for mail surveys.
6. Use tokens or money incentives.

Careful use of these techniques will increase the response rates of surveys
and help avoid the problems of nonresponse error.

Observational Response Errors. These consist of interviewing errors,
recording errors, and processing errors. Usually, these errors occur
because inaccurate information is gathered from the respondent or the
wrong information is recorded. In some cases error is also introduced
during the editing, coding, tabulating, and processing of the data. These
types of errors may be the most dangerous because, unlike nonobservational errors, observational errors cannot be predicted. Careful training,
supervision, monitoring, and editing are required to minimize this type
of error.

A final type of error that should be mentioned is cheating. *Cheating*
is the deliberate falsification of information by the interviewer. To avoid
this problem, adequate control and supervision must be exercised.

SUMMARY

Once a data-gathering instrument is designed and the appropriate sample
frame and size are selected (see chapter 7), it is time to field the instrument and execute the data-gathering process. To accomplish this smoothly
and with a minimum of error, preplanning is necessary. Proper budgeting
and personnel recruitment lead the list of planning activities for the
well-executed field service effort. Interviewers should be trained, briefed,
and well-supervised to obtain optimum results.

The interviewing relationship requires special attention to ensure proper rapport and understanding between the interviewer and the respondent. Specific guidelines should be followed by interviewers depending on the type of interview being conducted.

General rules of interviewing include maintaining security of the survey, providing proper training and briefing sessions, maintaining close supervision, adhering to specific study specifications, following all study procedures and instructions, keeping accurate records, completing assignments on time, working efficiently, probing appropriately, and maintaining clarity.

chapter seven

Sampling Methods and Sample Size

In the course of most research projects the time usually comes when estimates must be made about the characteristics or attitudes of a large group. The total of the study group of interest is called the *population* or *universe*. For example, all of the registered Republicans in Jefferson County or all of the heads of households in Madison, Indiana, would each constitute a universe. Once the study universe is decided on, several courses of action might be taken. First, the decision might be made to survey all of the entites in the universe. If all of the members of the selected universe are surveyed, this is called a *census*. With a census direct, straightforward information is obtained concerning the specific universe parameters or characteristics. A second course of action would be to survey a sample of the universe. *Sample* refers to the group surveyed whenever the survey is not administered to all members of the population. The process of selecting a smaller group of people with the same characteristics and preferences as the total group from which it is drawn is called *sampling*. The first basic requirement in sampling is that each individual in a population has an equal chance of being selected for the sample. When sampling is employed, information concerning the specific universe parameters or characteristics is inferred. The more representative the sample, the more accurate and representative the references made about the population will be. Most surveys are administered to some type of sample of the universe for the sake of simplicity and economy.

WHY SAMPLING?

There are many reasons for selecting a sampling technique over a census. In most cases the study objects of interest are represented by a large universe. This fact alone gives rise to many advantages of sampling. The most significant are:

1. *Cost savings*. Sampling a portion of the universe minimizes the field service costs associated with the survey.
2. *Time economy*. Information can be collected, processed, and analyzed much more quickly when a sample is utilized rather than a census. This saves additional money and helps ensure that the information is not obsolete by the time it is available to answer the research question.
3. *More in-depth information*. The act of sampling affords the researcher greater opportunity to carry the investigation in more depth to a smaller number of select population members. This may be done in the form of focus groups, panels, personal interviews, telephone interviews, or mail surveys.
4. *Less error*. A major problem in survey data collection comes about as the result of nonsampling errors. Greater overall accuracy can be gained by a better trained and supervised field service group.
5. *Greater practicality*. A census would not be practical for testing products from an assembly line or when the testing involves the destruction of the product, as with durability or safety tests.
6. *Greater security*. This is particularly true if a firm is researching a new product or concept. Sampling is preferred for keeping the product or concept a secret as long as possible.

SAMPLING DECISION MODEL

Step 1

Once the researcher has decided to apply sampling technique rather than a census, several important sampling decisions must be made. The first decision is to define the population or universe. Since sampling is designed to gather data from a specific population, it is extremely important for the universe to be identified accurately. Often this universe is called a *target population* because of the importance of focusing in on exactly who the study objects are and where they are located. Usually, any effort expended to do a first-rate job of identifying the population pays generous dividends later in terms of accurate and appropriate data. Clues to identifying the target population can be found in the research objectives. Well-thought-out research objectives will define the target population. The research questions and research hypotheses generated from them should refine the definition of the target population. The sample must be reduced to the most appropriate common denominator.

74

Do the research objectives require individuals, households, purchase decision makers, product users? Professional staff experience and insight are required to properly specify the target population.

Step 2

The second step in the sampling decision model is to determine the sampling frame. The *sampling frame* is a listing of the members of the target population that can be used to create or draw the sample. It might be a directory, subscriber list, customer list, or membership roster. In some cases, the sampling frame coincides with the target population and includes everyone in the population. However, this ideal situation is rare. Sample lists or frames can be purchased from companies specializing in sample preparation from third parties, or they can be put together by combining several sources. Because of the incompleteness of sampling frames, several discrepancies develop. Sometimes the sample frame is made up of the subjects of interest but is smaller than the total population. As a result, certain elements of the population are omitted from the survey. In other cases, the sample frame includes all members of the population but is larger than the population. Duplications or inappropriate units are included in the survey in these situations. A third situation occurs when some elements of the population fall in the sampling frame and when some elements of the sampling frame are in the population. In this case, both omissions and extraneous inclusions occur.

Step 3

The third step in the sampling decision model is to select the sampling method. This decision logically follows the decisions to determine the target population and the sampling frame. The initial consideration in the selection of a sample is whether or not to employ a probability sampling procedure or a nonprobability sampling procedure.

Probability Sampling. Probability samples are simply those samples for which each element has a known chance to be included. With nonprobability samples there is no way to estimate the probability of any given element being included in the sample. With probability sampling a chance or random procedure is utilized to select the study elements. The researcher preselects the respondents in a mathematical way so that all individuals in the universe have an equal or known chance of being selected. From a statistical point of view, probability sampling is preferred because it allows for a calculation of the sampling error. Probability sampling procedures tend to be more objective and permit the use of statistical techniques. From an operational perspective, nonprobability sampling offers some advantage. Also, the fact that a sample is a probability sample does not ensure that it will be any more representative than a nonprobability sample. The most commonly used probability samples are simple random samples, stratified samples, cluster samples, and systematic samples.

- A *simple random sample* allows each element of the population an equal and known chance of being selected as part of the sample. The implementation is often accomplished by using a table of random numbers. An example is provided in appendix D. A table of random numbers is simply a long list of numbers configured by randomly selecting a number from zero to nine. Knowledge of a string of any ten numbers will give no knowledge of what the next one might be. A table of random numbers may be entered at any point and appropriate random sample elements selected. A common analogy for a random sample is the traditional drawing of a sample from a fishbowl.

- When subgroups of the population are of special interest to the researcher, a *stratified sample* may serve better than a simple random sample. A stratified sample is characterized by the fact that the total population is divided into mutually exclusive subgroups and a simple random sample is chosen from each subgroup. This is a modified type of random sample. A stratified sample is simply drawn from each group separately to ensure that each is proportionally requested. The method of creating a stratified sample ensures that all important subgroups are represented in the sample. The stratified random sampling technique is good for classifying consumers by various demographic factors. The stratified samples can be divided into proportionately stratified samples or into disproportionately stratified samples. A proportionately stratified sample allows for a breakdown where the number of items randomly selected in each subgroup is proportionate to their numbering in the total population. A disproportionately stratified sample is a sample where the allocation of sample elements is not established according to relative proportion. This may result in equal elements per subgroup or it may result in the greater sampling of the subgroups that have the greater potential for variability. This, however, requires prior knowledge of the characteristics of the population. Just as with a simple random sample, there can be no stratified sample if there is no available frame of elements of the population that breaks down the population into the appropriate subgroups.

- In some cases when stratified sampling is not possible or feasible, *cluster sampling* can be utilized. The first step in selecting a cluster is the same as for a stratified sample; the population is divided into mutually exclusive subgroups. However, the next step involves the selection of a random sample of subgroups rather than a random sample from each subgroup. Cluster sampling may not be as statistically efficient as a stratified sample; however, it is usually more procedurally efficient in terms of cost and time. Cluster sampling is often associated with *area sampling,* in which each cluster is a different geographic area, census tract, block, or other division.

• A fourth technique of probability sampling is called *systematic sampling*. In this method, every element has a known but not equal chance of being selected. Systematic sampling is an attempt to increase the efficiency of the sample at favorable costs. A systematic sample is initiated by randomly selecting a digit, *n*, and then selecting a sample element at every *n*th interval, depending on the size of the population and the sample size requirement. This method is often used when selecting samples from large directories. Some loss of statistical efficiency can occur with systematic samples, particularly if there are hidden periodic sequences that cause some systematic variances to occur at the intervals selected.

Nonprobability Samples. Nonprobability samples are defined as any sampling techniques that do not involve the selection of sample elements by chance. The choices are made by convenience, expert judgment, or other criteria. Consequently, an estimate of the sampling error cannot be made. The main concern for choosing an appropriate sample is how representative it is, not whether it is a probability or nonprobability sample. Well-designed nonprobability samples can be as representative as probability samples. The most commonly utilized nonprobability sampling techniques are convenience sampling, judgment sampling, and quota sampling.

• The least expensive and least time-consuming of sampling techniques is generally considered to be a *convenience sample,* which is any process that quickly and easily selects sample elements. The sample element close at hand is chosen and surveyed in the application of this technique. Man-on-the-street interviews are examples of this type of sampling. The greatest problem with convenience sampling is the inability to know if the sample is representative of the target population. Consequently, one cannot generalize from the sample to the target population with a high degree of confidence.

• The representativeness of a *judgment sample* obviously depends on the skill, insight, and experience of the one choosing the sample. Although a judgment sample is a subjective approach to sampling, the knowledge and experience of a professional researcher can create a very representative sample. This is particularly true in industrial studies where a knowledge of the industry dynamics and decision-making procedures is necessary to identify the correct respondents. In the area of polling expert opinion, judgment samples can be very effective. Even though judgment samples are more restrictive and generally more representative than convenience samples, they have the same weakness of not permitting direct generalization of conclusions derived to a target population.

• The third type of nonprobability sampling, *quota sampling,* is similar in some respects to stratified and cluster sampling. In quota sampling the researcher divides the target population into a number of subgroups. Then, using his or her best judgment, the researcher selects quotas for each subgroup. The quota method takes great effort to obtain a representative sample by dividing the population and assigning appropriate quotas based on prior knowledge and understanding of the characteristics of the population. Quota sampling is often used in market research projects.

Step 4

Once the researcher has selected the appropriate sampling procedure, a decision must be made about the actual sample size. This is a very important decision in the research process. There are many factors to be considered. Appendix D provides details about how to evaluate and determine actual sample size. However, in this section tables are provided to help you to select sample size for situations where you are measuring attitudes or variables at various levels of confidence.

The size of the sample, then, will also be a function of the accuracy of the sample. Two criteria are used in measuring the accuracy of the sample. One is called the margin of error and the other is the level of confidence. The *margin of error* is determined as the tolerated error range (also known as sample precision), and the *level of confidence* is the probability that the sample will fall within that tolerated error range. A margin of error of 5 percent, for example, means that out of all possible samples of a certain determined size of coin flips, 95 percent will differ from the actual population by no more than five percentage points. It should be noted that the other 5 percent won't be much further off either.

Ultimately, sample size determination is a reflection of the value of the information sought. Scientific journals require reported results that fall in the 95-to-99-percent confidence levels. When the risk inolved in the decision alternatives is high, then the 95-to-99-percent confidence levels will be required. The sampling of well-known television ratings is at the 66-percent confidence level. The margin of error in these ratings is believed to be far too great for the advertising decisions that are based on this result. Even low-budget studies, with low-risk decision alternatives that serve as a glimpse into the market environment, should never consider less than an 85-to-90-percent confidence level. The 95-percent confidence level is suggested for most research.

The procedures in appendix D will give greater definition to developing accurate sample sizes for different populations. However table 7–1, based on many studies from research institutions, provides guidelines for determining sample size from different types of populations.[1]

Table 7–1. Typical Sample Sizes for Consumer and
Institutional Population Studies

Number of Subgroups	Consumer or Households		Institutions	
	National	Regional or Special	National	Regional or Special
0–4	850–1500	250–500	150–500	50–200
5–10	1500–2500	500–1000	350–1000	150–500
Over 10	2500+	1000+	1000+	1000+

The number of subgroups required for a sample may be known or may require some preliminary investigation or pretesting.

The main factors that have a direct influence on the size of the sample are:

1. *The desired degree of confidence associated with the estimate.* In other words, how confident does the researcher want to be in the results of the survey? If the researcher wants 100-percent confidence, he or she must take a census. The more confident a researcher wants to be, the larger the sample should be. This confidence is usually expressed in terms of 90, 95, or 99 percent.

2. *The size of the error the researcher is wiling to accept.* This width of the interval relates to the precision desired from the estimate. The greater the precision, or rather the smaller the plus-or-minus fluctuation around the sample mean, the larger the sample requirement.

The degree of confidence and margin of error are interrelated. One may be increased, but only at the expense of the other.

In probability sampling, the size of the sample is more closely associated with the precision of the estimate and the variation of the population than the overall size of the population. Many people are quite surprised that the size of the population does not play a larger role in determining sample size for probability sampling. However, the degree of precision and variability of the sample becomes a function of the sample size. Once the sample size reaches a certain level, the precision and confidence level will remain constant, even if the population is increased.

It should be noted that the statistical methods of establishing sample size discussed above apply only to probability samples. In the case of nonprobability samples, the chance of any element of the population being chosen for the sample is unknown. Consequently, the principles of normal distribution and the central limit theorem do not apply. This eliminates the possibility of being able to use the formulas discussed in this chapter or the tables in appendix D to establish sample size.

The choice of sample size for a nonprobability sample is made on a subjective basis. This should not concern the researcher too much because many of the estimates made to calculate sample size for probability samples are also made on a subjective basis. In nonprobability samples, size is determined by the insight, judgment, experience,or financial resources of the researcher. The important thing about a sample is that it should be representative, not that it should be statistically derived. There are a number of rules of thumb, such as "You reach diminishing benefits with samples greater than 300," "No sample should be smaller than 40," or "A good sample is about 10 percent of the population." However, the final decision about the sample size depends on whether it is felt by the researcher or sponsor to be representative of the population.

Besides judgment, available funds, and rules of thumb, there are other methods of determining sample size. One is the anticipated cross-classification of the data. If several demographic attributes or variables are going to be utilized, then concern must be given to the size of the cells of the cross-tabulation tables. The more cells in the table, the larger the sample size must be. Another consideration related to sample size is the form of analysis that the data will undergo. Certain types of analysis, such as multidimensional scaling, will require larger sample sizes. Another consideration is the nature of the research being conducted. Exploratory research will generally require smaller samples than descriptive or substantive research. Another consideration is the expected completion rate of the survey. The lower the expected completion rate, the larger the sample must be.

Step 5

Once the target population has been identified, an appropriate sampling frame determined or compiled, all sampling procedures selected, and a sample size determined, it is time for the final step in the sampling decision model. The sampling process should be executed in an efficient and professional way, as was described in chapter 6.

Whether a sample is a probability sample or a nonprobability sample, it is important to obtain as much representative information and eliminate as much sampling and nonsampling error as possible. Generally speaking, the sample size should be increased whenever the population exhibits high variability or whenever high levels of confidence and precision are required.

SUMMARY

This chapter has presented the important aspects of sampling. The right size sample drawn in the right way is determined by the nature of the research project. In some projects it is a critical decision area because of costs and the need to draw inferences to the population from which the sample comes.

NOTES

1. SEYMOUR SUDMAN, *Applied Sampling* (New York: Academic Press, 1976).

chapter eight

Data Analysis and Interpretation

An understanding of the basic principles of data analysis and interpretation is important to the decision maker for several reasons. Initially, it enables the decision maker to uncover information and insights that otherwise would not be available. Next, this understanding furnishes checks to help avoid erroneous judgments and conclusions. Likewise, it provides a background from which to evaluate the analyses and interpretations made by others. Finally, an understanding of the power and purpose of individual analytical techniques can constructively influence the initial input that affects the research objectives and research design.[1]

ANALYSIS AND
INTERPRETATION PRINCIPLES

It should be pointed out that the analysis of data does not in and of itself provide the decision-making information that is sought. Data interpretation is necessary. Data interpretation is the assignment of meaning to raw data. Data interpretation will aid in the evaluation of decision alternatives. The purpose of analysis is the reduction of data to intelligible and interpretable form so that relationships among variables relating to the research questions can be identified, studied, and tested. The analysis, then, is the categorizing, ordering, manipulating, and summarizing of data. The interpretation takes the results of the analysis, makes inferences relative to the problem or questions being studied, and then draws conclusions about these relations. The interpretation involves the search for meaning and implications of the results. A meaningful analysis and interpretation will require the careful mixing of judgment, informed insight, statistical procedures, and a thorough knowledge of the decision alternatives under consideration.

At the heart of the analysis are the statistical procedures used. There are many kinds of statistical methods. The major forms include frequency (percentage) distributions, graphic analyses, measures of central tendency and variability (median, mean, and mode), measures of relations (product-moment correlations, rank order correlation coefficients), analysis of differences (whether differences in percentages, means, ranges, correlations, or variances), analysis of variance (measuring the cause of variance among dependent variables and between independent variables), profile analysis (a set of measures describing a group), and, finally, multivariate (multiple variable) analysis. *Multivariate analysis* describes a family of analytic methods that serve to simultaneously analyze a certain number of independent variables with a certain number of dependent variables. Multivariate methods attempt to more closely approximate behavioral or attitudinal reality.

STATISTICS IN PLAIN LANGUAGE

Statistics serve the purpose of measurement. It has been explained that measurement consists of the assignment of numbers to attitudes, behaviors, or happenings, which are then systematically quantified, compared, and analyzed. Fred N. Kerlinger explains that the basic principle behind the use of statistical measures is comparing obtained results with chance expectation.[2] In other words, the results obtained will point out the significance to be given to certain variables that might not have been expected if the analysis had been left to chance or simple intuition. This point undergirds the basic purpose of research, which is the reduction of error in decision making.

Statistics, therefore, serve to reduce large quantities of data to understandable and manageable form. Kerlinger defines a *statistic* as a measure calculated from a sample. He points out that a statistic differs from a *parameter*, which is the actual population value on which the sample is based. Statistics allow conclusions to be drawn on total populations without the unwieldy task of measuring a total population. Means, modes, medians, variances, standard deviations, percentiles, and so on, calculated from samples, are statistics. It follows that the second function of statistics is to aid in the study of populations and samples. The third function served by statistics, therefore, is to aid in decision making by presenting data in manageable and palatable form. Finally, statistics serve to aid in making reliable inferences from observational data, which is tied directly to the purpose of aiding in decision making.[3]

While the analysis of statistics is the reduction of data to intelligible form, the interpretation of the results of the analysis involves the search for meaning and implications of the results. Statistical inference underlies the interpretation. Inferences from statistics are usually made from samples to populations. Inferences also serve the important function of determining presumed effects of relationships between variables. The central purpose of statistics is to serve as an aid in making inferences.[4] This is fundamental to the central purpose of research designs and methodologies. Reducing the error in decision making flows from drawing inferences from manageable data, which allows for the determination of relationships that otherwise would not be readily apparent.[5]

DATA ANALYSIS PROCESS

The form of data analysis developed for each study will be unique, to ensure the best fit for the specific purposes of the individual study. Each study will have a logical flow process, which becomes the framework of the analysis. Once data are collected, whether by interviews or other means, they are edited and coded. Questions are then tabulated. After questions are tabulated, subgroups in the sample are tabulated. This is also known as *cross-tabulation*. Tabulations and cross-tabulations are simple percentages assigned to the responses given for each question. This step will also include any other simple statistics that might be performed, such as determining the differences between mean (or average) scores. Next comes the execution of correlation analysis, which is followed by multivariate analysis. The results from tabulations, cross-tabulations, correlations, and multivariate techniques are then synthesized and interpreted in a final results summary, ready for presentation.

The analytic process begins with editing and coding. The purpose of editing in this process is to identify omissions, ambiguities, and errors in responses. Problems identified at this point are returned to their sources for correction and/or clarification. Coding involves the assignment of coded numbers to the responses to each question, which prepares the data for computerization. Tabulations usually consist of determining the percentage and/or the average scores for each question. The purpose of cross-tabulations is not to repeat the analysis of a single question, but to extend it to each of the subgroups in the sample. For example, from the total sample scores it might be learned that 80 percent of the respondents prefer a certain product. However, the cross-tabulation might reveal that only 60 percent of those under twenty-four years of age prefer it and 95 percent of those thirty-five to forty-nine years of age prefer it.

Correlations establish a relationship between any two intervally scaled variables. Variables can be negatively and positively correlated. Correlation scores range from $+1.00$ to -1.00, with 1.00 (or -1.00) indicating a perfect relation and 0 indicating no relation at all. Generally, depending on sample size, two variables are said to be slightly correlated when the correlation scores are between 0.21 and 0.35. Moderate degrees of correlation are generally associated with scores of 0.36 through 0.55. High degrees of correlation would be 0.56 through 0.75. Extremely high degrees of correlation would be associated with the scores 0.76 through 0.99. When two variables are positively correlated, it means that when one variable tends to increase in value, importance, or preference, the other will likewise tend to increase. When two variables are negatively (or inversely) correlated, it means that when one variable tends to increase in value, the other decreases, and vice versa. One example might be that the purchase selection factor of the importance of product quality is inversely correlated to the importance of cost savings; as the quality of the product increases, the importance of cost savings to the consumer decreases.

MULTIVARIATE
ANALYTIC TECHNIQUES

Multivariate (multiple variable) analysis refers to the statistical methods that simultaneously analyze multiple measurements of attitudes, attributes, or behaviors. Multivariate techniques are simply extensions of univariate techniques (analysis of single variable distributions) and bivariate techniques (two variable methods such as cross-tabulations, correlations, and simple regression). For a research project to terminate prior to employing multivariate techniques assumes that the purpose of the research was only to identify the variables, or that the importance of the results for the decision information required lay only in the establishment of the differences between the variables. Multivariate techniques serve to determine the relationships that exist between multiple sets of variables. Multivariate methodologies are clearly required to adequately examine the multiple constraints and relationships among pertinent variables to obtain a more complete, realistic understanding of the market environment for decision making. A multivariate examination ensures that superficiality of results is avoided.

The satisfactory utilization of multivariate methods assumes a degree of understanding of the market dynamics or market behavior in order to conceptualize a realistic model. This relates to the first objective of the research process, which is to identify the variables. The identification of the variables whose relationships are to be measured is basic to an incisive multivariate approach. The nature and number of variables to be examined will determine what type of multivariate method will be utilized.

Multiple
Regression Analysis

Multiple regression analysis allows for the prediction of the level of magnitude of a phenemonon such as market size or market share. Multiple regression has as its objective the identification of the optimum simultaneous relationship that exists between the distribution of the predicted variable and those of the many causal variables.[6] For example, frequency of listenership to a particular radio station may well be a function of a number of marketing mix variables, such as the type of programming, listener loyalty, community promotionals, billboard advertising, disc jockey personality, and tastefulness of the commercials.

Multiple
Discriminate Analysis

Multiple discriminate analysis has as its objective the identification of key descriptors on which various predefined events will vary.[7] It might be learned from a discriminate analysis that middle-income families who work in a downtown area and who have school-age children might be expected to be the first to move into a new, rural, totally planned community housing development.

Canonical
Correlation Analysis

A canonical correlation analysis allows for the establishment of a predictive model that can simultaneously forecast or explain several phenomena based on an understanding of their correlates. The canonical correlation analysis differs from multiple regression analysis in that there is more than one predicted variable. Whereas family income and family size might be used to predict the number of credit cards a family might have (by using a multiple regression technique), the canonical correlation analysis would also be able to predict the average monthly charges on all of their credit cards.[8]

Factor Analysis

Kerlinger states that factor analysis might be called the queen of analytic techniques because of its power and elegance. Kerlinger describes factor analysis as a method for determining the number and nature of underlying variables among larger numbers of measures. It also serves to reduce large groups of complex variables to their underlying and predictive entities. Factor analytic techniques first gained prominence in psychological and psychiatric studies. For example, verbal ability, numerical ability, memory, abstract reasoning, and spatial reasoning have been found to underlie intelligence in some studies.[9]

The applications for factor analysis have been used extensively for behavioral and attitudinal studies in the marketplace. For example, a recent study that measured a large group of variables related to job satisfaction and morale among a certain group of engineers revealed that the ability to grow professionally was the single most important factor in morale and job satisfaction. This was followed closely by self-esteem as it related to the type of firm for which they worked. The analysis revealed five central factors, which in general terms, fit very closely to Maslow's hierarchy of organizational needs. Maslow's theory identifies a hierarchy in which human needs arrange themselves. Each need is prominent until satisfied, which leads to the next level of need. In sequence, Maslow's needs include physical needs (food, clothing, shelter); safety or security needs; social or affiliation needs; esteem needs; and self-actualization needs.[10] The analysis of job satisfaction and morale among engineers approximated each of Maslow's needs, but with a different and interesting order of prominence. Factors identified by this technique, therefore, have served as a new dimension of segmentation that focuses on shared agreement among respondents as the differentiation among the segments.

Multidimensional Scaling

Multidimensional scaling (MDS) addresses the problem of identifying the dimensions upon which customers perceive or evaluate phenomena (products, brands, or companies). MDS techniques result in perceptual "maps" that describe the "positioning" of companies or brands that are compared relative to the "position" they occupy in the minds of customers according to key attributes. These maps allow the decision maker to examine underlying criteria or dimensions that people utilize to form perceptions about similarities between and preferences among various products, services, brands, or companies. The question of positioning, as viewed by MDS and perceptual mapping, deals with how a firm compares to its competitors with respect to key attributes, what the ideal set of attributes sought by the customer might be, or what positioning or repositioning strategy should be developed for a specific sector of the marketplace.[11] A medium-sized bank might learn, for example, that the most effective way to compete for commercial loan business with larger, more prestigious banks with a wider range of services is to focus on the genuine concern communicated by loan supervisors as well as the expertise they develop in their knowledge of their clients' subsector of industry.

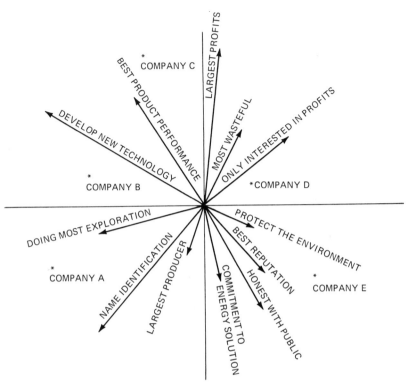

Figure 8.1

Cluster Analysis

The cluster analysis allows for the classification or segmentation of a large group of variables into homogeneous subgroups based on similarities on a profile of information. Cluster analysis allows for the description of typologies or profiles according to attitudes toward preferences, appeals, and so on, which might also include psychographic data. For example, this analysis might be used to describe psychographic profiles and interest in new transactional services among savings and loan customers.[12]

Conjoint Analysis

Conjoint measurement, also known as *trade-off analysis,* is used for evaluating judgmental data where choices between attributes are involved. It is more commonly used in measuring the trade-off values of purchase selection factor attributes. Specifically, conjoint analysis is concerned with the joint effect of two or more independent variables on the ordering of a dependent variable. In essence, this method allows a determination of how consumers value various levels of purchase criteria and the extent to which they might tend to forego a high level of one attribute in order to obtain a high level of another attribute. For example, the trade-off values of holding power, scent, nonstickiness, brand name, and price for hair spray might be cause for a conjoint evaluation.[13]

PRINCIPLES
OF MARKET ANALYSIS

The proper utilization of any analytical technique for decision making begins with a clear understanding and definition of the market to be examined. This will include the dimensions, interactions, and structure of the market environment. Market segmentation, market positioning, and current and potential market demand will be vital to the analysis of any market.

Kotler explains that a market for a product or service consists of those people with an actual or potential interest in the product or service, as well as the resources for obtaining the product or service.[14] The analysis and research application to be chosen not only must fit closely with this definition, but it must also serve to clarify and define its components as it reflects the individual market environment. Aaker and Day point out that the degree of interest in a product or service depends on the closeness of the match between the consumers' needs and the ability of the product or service to meet those needs.[15] Various techniques that measure interest, preferences, or importance of product or brand attributes have already been described. Once that is understood, the identification is made of the target market segments that provide the best fit for a product that already exists or that present the optimum potential for a product that can be developed. Once these data are developed, product, brand, or company "positioning" for each targeted segment is made. This process underlies the ongoing analysis of the change in the dynamics of the market environment and the assessment of opportunity based on current and projected trends. Analytical applications, viewed as a part of this process, thus become very practical and meaningful.

RESEARCH
STUDY APPLICATIONS

There is a wide range of research applications that provide the framework for data analysis, resulting in the decision-making information to effectively keep in touch with the shifts, changes, and emerging trends reflective of market needs and preferences. A few examples of applications include the following:

Concept/product testing. A concept or product test consists of evaluating consumer response to a new product or concept. This is often a part of the test market in the development of a new product. It is also used to determine how a product or service can best be positioned in a particular sector of the marketplace. For example, product testing would identify the consumer's perception of new products or services to be offered. It can also examine how users perceive a product's value as well as its attributes and benefits, or how perceived values and attributes relate to actual need and demand.

Tracking study. A tracking study is an ongoing periodic survey of prerecruited consumers who rate their use of various products or services. Specific preferences are measured and compared to evaluate changes in perceptions, preferences, and actual usage over time.

Product/brand/service usage. Product or brand usage studies serve to determine current demand for the various brands of a product or service. This type of approach may also determine which brand name has top-of-mind awareness in the consumers' minds or which they prefer, how often it is used, and why.

Advertising penetration. Advertising penetration analyses evaluate the message that is actually being communicated to the target audience. This type of study serves to determine if the intended message is understood, how persuasive it is, or how well it motivates. These studies may also evaluate the effectiveness of individual media for a particular target market.

Image evaluation. Image studies provide feedback relative to the image a company, product, or service has in the eyes of the consumers. Image studies may reveal what attributes a particular brand is perceived as having or determine its strengths and weaknesses.

Public opinion surveys. Public opinion studies determine the key issues in the minds of the public or specific customers (or investors), relative to specific issues, individuals, or business sectors. They reveal whether opinion is positive or negative, determine the degree of importance of specific issues, or evaluate awareness levels of key issues.

Copy testing. Copy testing allows for an evaluation of consumer response to advertising copy being considered. It determines how well the intended message is actually being communicated. Copy tests ensure that the wording is consistent with the language of the target audience. Copy testing is used most effectively in the conceptual stages of copy development to allow for consumer feedback on concepts portrayed by preliminary ad copy.

Test marketing/product placements. Product placements are a bit more extensive than product tests. Product tests take place in a controlled setting, such as in a shopping mall where consumers are recruited to test a product. In a product placement study, the product to be test marketed is placed with the consumer for a specific period of time to be used at home. A personal or telephone interview is used to record the specific detailed responses of the user to the product. This type of study will determine how consumers respond to a product that often has no name or packaging appeals associated with it.

Taste tests. Taste tests are conducted in a controlled environment where consumers are recruited, taste a product, and give their evaluations. Taste tests serve to determine the acceptance of a product without brand or packaging appeals relative to attributes of flavor, texture, aroma, and visual appeal. Taste tests may be conducted with variations of a single product or with samples of competitors' products tasted for comparison.

Market segmentation. Market segmentation of market targeting studies determine how a market is segmented by product usage, demand, or customer profiles. These studies usually develop demographic, psychographic, product preference, and lifestyle profiles of key market segments.

Media measurement. These studies determine what share of the market the medium being tested actually has and how a target market is identified demographicaly and psychographically. Media studies also evaluate preferences in programming as well as what promotional appeals are most effective in reaching and expanding a particular target audience.

Market feasibility. A market feasibility study analyzes the market demand for a new product, brand, or service. This type of study usually evaluates potential market size and determines what kind of demand might be expected, what market dynamics are interacting, and what market segments might be most receptive to the introduction of a new product or brand. Feasibility studies may also determine market feedback relative to similar products or services, attributes sought, and pricing and packaging perspectives.

Location studies. For local-customer-intensive businesses, the location must be determined. Location studies serve to evaluate the size of the potential market surrounding a proposed location and whether local demand will support the facility.

Market share/market size studies. Market share/market size studies determine what products are being purchased at what volume and the actual sales being realized by each competitor. These studies usually also identify and determine the strength of new firms that have recently entered the market in a strong growth mode.

Competitive analysis. A competitive analysis is often part of a market share/market size study. It consists of an evaluation of the strengths and weaknesses of competitors. It may also include pertinent data about locations, sales approaches, and the extent of product lines and manufacturing capabilities.

Positioning studies. Positioning studies evaluate how leading companies or brands are viewed by consumers as far as key product or image attributes are concerned. This type of study will evaluate perceived strengths and weaknesses of each, and will determine key attributes that consumers associate with their idea of an "ideal" supplier of a particular product or service.

TECHNOLOGICAL
PERSPECTIVES AND RESEARCH

Technological developments in the last two decades have added greatly to the speed, accuracy, and range of techniques available for the processing and manipulation of data for decision making. Advancements in microprocessing and software, as well as impressive cost reductions, are putting some degree of internal computing capability within the reach of virtually every moderately sized business in the United States. Standardized programs for mainframe computers have been developed with simple instructions and steps for very sophisticated analytical techniques. These standardized programs have added greatly to the accessibility and subsequent wide use of all levels of statistical procedures. The incredible speed, economy, and availability of computer technology has resulted in data analysis for decision making being available to businesses and departments of almost every size. The Statistical Analysis System (SAS) and the Statistical Package for Social Sciences (SPSS) are two very popular and easy-to-use programs that include a wide range of univariate, bivariate, and multivariate analytical techniques.

Computer terminals provide access to computer time-sharing through which special programs, data storage, or standard statistical packages (such as SAS or SPSS) may be available. Computer terminals also give access to a growing array of on-line data bases available in a wide variety of industries.

New small-business computers (microprocessors) are beginning to carry software package options for limited types of statistical analyses. These internal capabilities will allow for better access and analysis of sales trends, inventories, customer segmentation data, and so forth.

Larger market research firms have telephone interviewers who work at cathode ray tube (CRT) screens while interviewing respondents. The questionnaire is coded into the computer and responses to each question are keyed into the system instead of being written on a printed questionnaire, thus eliminating the coding and keypunching or data entry steps that are normally required. This advancement allows for much quicker turnaround in the processed data needed for analysis. Many feel this advancement alone will change the nature of the data gathering business within the next decade. Other technological entries into the business of research include grocery checkout scanners and cable television ad comparison tests. Adtel and Behaviorscan are but two of these new technologies sweeping the industry. These new technologies carry special importance to the quality and accuracy of information available for decision making. More limitations to understanding markets and actual market needs will continue to be overcome. The importance of the information included in the planning process will continue to increase. The competitive edge will be held by those who understand and make effective use of these developing technologies and information resources.

SUMMARY

Decision-making information is the result of the systematic specification, gathering, analysis, and interpretation of data. The purpose of the analysis is the reduction of data to intelligible and interpretable form. The interpretation of data consists of the search for the meaning and implications of the results of the analysis. The statistical methods chosen to form the basis of the analysis must provide measures that are an appropriate fit to the decision alternative being evaluated. To be meaningful, the analysis and interpretation will require a correct blending of judgment, informed insight, well-designed statistical procedures, and a thorough knowledge of the decision alternatives under consideration.

NOTES

1. DAVID A. AAKER and GEORGE S. DAY, *Marketing Research: Private and Public Sector Dimensions* (New York: John Wiley, 1980).

2. FRED N. KERLINGER, *Foundations of Behavioral Research* (New York: Holt, Rinehart and Winston, 1973).

3. Ibid.

4. Ibid.

5. Ibid.

6. JOSEPH F. HAIR, JR., ROLPH E. ANDERSON, RONALD L. TATHAM and BERNIE J. GRABLOWSKY, *Multivariate Data Analysis with Readings* (Tulsa: Penwell Publishing Company, 1979).

7. Ibid.

8. Ibid.

9. KERLINGER.

10. ABRAHAM H. MASLOW, *Motivation and Personality* (New York: Harper & Row, 1954).

11. AAKER and DAY.

12. HAIR, et al.

13. HAIR, et al.

14. PHILIP KOTLER, *Marketing for Non-Profit Organizations* (Englewood Cliffs, N.J.: Prentice-Hall, 1975).

15. AAKER and DAY.

chapter nine

The Research Report

This chapter discusses the essentials of preparing the research report. The basic purpose of the research report is to communicate the results, conclusions, and recommendations of the research project. (If a project encompasses several phases or a long period of time, progress reports are normally sent to the purchasers or users of the research to inform them of the progress to date on a given project.) The key word in the preceding statement of purpose is *communicate*. The report must be an effective tool of communication not only to accurately present the findings and conclusions, but also to stimulate the reader to take some managerial action. The research project was predicated on the need for information to aid in the decision-making process. Now the cycle is complete, and the report must address that decision and recommend a course of action in view of the research findings. The user or purchaser of the information must decide whether or not to heed the advice given in the report, but the actions recommended by the researcher must be communicated.

There are two basic types of research reports: the technical report and the popular report. Each type makes some assumptions about the interests and backgrounds of the potential readers. The type of report prepared should be based on an analysis of the audience for which it is designed.

THE TECHNICAL
RESEARCH REPORT

A technical report assumes that the readers have a background in research methodology and are interested in the details of research design, sampling design, statistical methods, and so on. The readers are interested in a full presentation and a detailed discussion of each of the steps in the research project. They are in the position of being able to evaluate the appropriateness and accuracy with which each step was carried out. The writer can assume that the more technical language of research design and analysis will be understood by the reader.

If this type of report is prepared, it should present a detailed account of each step in the project, including copies of questionnaires and perhaps computer printouts of results. This would be especially needed where statistical tests were performed on the data. This type of report is most likely to be used when it will become a part of a series of studies (referred to as *tracking studies*) so that the methodology can be duplicated in subsequent projects.

THE MANAGEMENT REPORT

The management report is designed for a different audience. The assumption is made that the readers are not interested in details about the research techniques but are mainly interested in the findings. This is the most typical type of report read by business executives. The major interests of these readers are in the findings and the application of the findings to the decisions to be made in a given situation.

The writing style is designed for rapid reading and comprehension of the key findings of the research. The report is nontechnical and normally makes more use of pictures and graphs and less use of detailed tables. Short, precise statements of findings, conclusions, and recommendations are used along with hyphens, asterisks, and numbers to emphasize important points.

REPORT FORMAT

While there is no standardized reporting format used in all research reports, the following outline gives the elements normally included in the popular report:

1. Title page
2. Tables of contents, charts, and illustrations

3. Introduction
4. Executive summary or highlights
5. Conclusions and recommendations
6. Complete findings of the study
7. Supporting charts and tables
8. Appendixes

Title page. The title page should tell the reader four things: (1) the subject of the study, (2) for whom it was prepared, (3) by whom it was prepared, and (4) the date of the study. This title page may also bear the logo of the preparing organization if the project is completed by an outside organization.

Table of contents. A good rule to follow for including tables of contents, charts, and illustrations is to consider the length of the report. If the report is only ten to twelve pages long, then a table of contents is not necessary. For longer reports, tables of contents, charts, and illustrations are usually included to enable the readers to locate the sections or illustrations in the report to which they want to refer at a given time.

Introduction. The introduction to the report should refer the reader to the basic purpose of the research and the specific objectives that were agreed upon in the research proposal. It will usually contain statements of limitations and a brief statement of research methodology, such as from whom the data were collected, when, how, and how many respondents were surveyed if primary data were collected. The introduction, in effect, sets forth the information needed to help the reader understand the context in which the data were collected.

Executive summary. The executive summary of the research report presents the highlights in a straightforward and precise manner. This summary is usually organized by topics investigated or by questions that must be answered before a decision is made.

This may be the only section read by some executives, so enough detailed statements of major issues must be given to arm them with the basic facts that emerged from the study. It should be strong enough to permit the reader to get the essence of the findings without assuming that a detailed study of the report will be made by every reader.

Conclusions and recommendations. As mentioned earlier, the research culminates with the statements given in reference to the decisions to be made based on the results of the research. The researcher's role is not just to present the facts, but also to draw conclusions on the basis of the findings and to make recommendations on the basis of these conclusions. The reader should be presented with a set of conclusions and recommendations for managerial action. While no researcher can force a manager to act on a set of recommendations, he or she should know enough about the decision and the data collected to recommend a course of action. That is what the researcher is being paid for! To simply present the facts and offer no recommendations is to lose the advantage gained by having someone who is not responsible for making the decision suggest at least some alternative actions. The decision maker still has to "drive the car," but the one who just read the "road map" can surely offer some suggestions about which way to go!

Findings. This section of the report contains the detailed findings of the study. A great deal of detail is given in this section, with supporting graphs and charts included both as a reference and as a source of support for the statements made in the narrative. This is normally the largest section of the report and should be organized in a logical way. A topically organized format lends itself to ease of both preparation and reading. The major topics related to each research objective are presented so that the reader is taken in a step-by-step progression through all of the findings of the study.

Supporting charts and tables. Since many computer services offer reductions of computer printouts, these are often included in a section of the report. The reader can then examine all the data analyzed through the computer program for a more detailed study of the findings. This also permits validation of the conclusions and recommendations made by the researcher.

Many statistical packages provide all of the accompanying analysis in the output, such as cell frequencies, probabilities of occurrence under a null hypothesis, standard errors, and so on. These can be examined for appropriateness of use in subsequent analyses if they are included in the report.

Appendixes. The appendixes can be used to present copies of questionnaires used in the study, more detailed secondary data, or any other type of data or material that might be helpful to the user of the report. In one study of a new outdoor recreational concept, articles on innovative recreational concepts that had been introduced previously were given. This is an example of how appendixes can be used. The researcher should avoid any attempt to pad or build up the size of a report by using appendixes. This only takes away from the communicative force of the body of the report.

ORAL REPORTS

Another effective way to convey the results of a study is with an oral presentation. The authors *do not* recommend this as a substitute for a written report, but only as a supplement to the written document. If the oral presentation is done effectively, it becomes a communication tool to reinforce what is given in the written report.

In many cases the oral report becomes a technique to communicate results to key executives who might not otherwise have interests or access to those who have been collecting data outside the organization.

With today's audiovisual technology, no oral report should fail to use these aids in the oral presentation. There is plenty of evidence to suggest that we remember more of what we *see* and *hear* than what we read. Slides and transparencies can be prepared at modest cost and greatly add to the impact of the presentation.

PRESENTING
STATISTICAL DATA

Two methods are used to present statistical data: tables and graphs. Both of these methods are commonly used in research reports, depending on the type of data or the emphasis the researcher wishes to place on a given set of data.

Tables. A statistical table is a method of presenting and arranging data that have been broken down by one or more systems of classification. *Analytical tables* are designed to aid in a formal analysis of interrelationships between variables. A *reference table* is designed to be a repository of statistical data. The distinction between these two types of data is their intended use and not their construction. Table 9–1 is an example of an analytical table. It was prepared to analyze differences in preferences based on the age of the respondents. Table 9–2 is a reference table, prepared to report to the reader the number of respondents of each sex that were interviewed. In preparing tables, care should be taken to include proper headings, notes about discrepancies (percentages that add up to more than 100, for example), and sources of data. This helps the reader interpret the data contained in the tables.

Table 9–1. Preferences for Motel-Related Restaurants by Age of Traveler*

	PREFERENCE**				
	Prefer Motel Restaurants		Prefer Non-Motel Restaurants		Totals by Age
	Number	Percentage	Number	Percentage	
Under 25	7	5.5%	130	45.3%	137
25–34	13	10.3%	62	21.6%	75
35–44	29	23.0%	38	13.2%	67
45–54	33	26.2%	35	12.1%	68
Over 55	44	34.9%	22	7.7%	66
Total	126	99.9%	287	100.0%	413

*Source: Survey data.
**Preference was defined as where they would eat if they were traveling and staying at a motel with a restaurant.

Table 9–2.

| | SEX OF TRAVELERS* | |
	Number	Percentage
Male	206	49.8%
Female	207	50.2%
Total	413	100.0%

*Source: Survey data.

Graphic presentation. There are many types of graphs that can aid in presenting data. Two of the most commonly used are bar charts and pie charts. These add a visual magnitude to the presentation of the data.

Bar charts are easily constructed and can be readily interpreted even by those not familiar with charts. They are especially useful in showing changes between time periods for a set of variables, as shown in Figure 9.1. From this chart you can easily see the increase in the sales of chicken sandwiches over the three-year period.

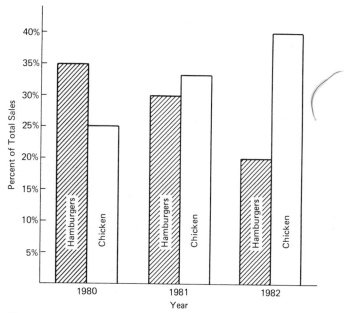

Figure 9.1

A pie chart is another useful graph in marketing studies, especially when showing market share. Figure 9.2 presents a sample pie chart. Adding color to highlight certain sections increases the visual impact of pie charts. This also permits identification of different shares held by different competitors.

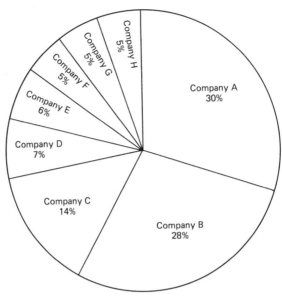

Figure 9.2

SUMMARY

This chapter has presented a brief overview of the steps involved in preparing a research report. (A copy of an actual report is included in appendix E.) The research report is not only a communication tool, but it is also a source document for future reference. The preparation of the report provides the researcher with the major vehicle to communicate research findings to management and to display the results of the work that went into completing the project.

Glossary

Accuracy: The closeness of the sample value to the true value.

Alpha error (or Type I Error): An error in hypothesis testing when the correct or true hypothesis is rejected.

Alternative hypothesis: The hypothesis that is accepted if the null hypothesis is rejected. There may be more than one alternative hypothesis.

Analysis: The process of extracting meaningful information out of raw survey data. *Analysis* literally means to break down into parts for the purpose of understanding.

Attitude: An enduring set of beliefs, feelings, and action tendencies toward an aspect of the individual's world.

Attribute: A characteristic of an object that does not have magnitude but only one direction.

Average deviation: The sum of the numbers' difference (from the mean) divided by the mean.

Beta error (or Type II Error): An error in hypothesis testing when the false hypothesis is accepted.

Bias: A systematic discrepancy in the true value and the sample value.

Causal research: A research study that attempts to specify or quantify the nature of the relationship between two or more variables in a model.

Census: A research process in which every element in the group or population of interest is surveyed.

Central tendency, measure of: Statistics used to indicate averages. The most commonly used are the mean, median, and mode.

Cluster analysis: The process of separating objects or variables into relatively homogeneous groups for purposes of statistical analysis.

Cluster sample design (also called Multistage): A procedure of selection in which the elements for the sample are chosen from the population in groups rather than individual sample elements.

Coding: The process of establishing categories for survey questions to which the responses are assigned. Multiple-choice and dichotomous questions are established at the time the questionnaire is formulated. Open-ended questions must be established after responses are collected.

Comparative rating scale: An attitude measure that asks the respondent to evaluate an object in direct reference to a specific standard.

Concurrent validity: The extent to which one measure can be used to estimate the current level on another variable.

Confidence interval: The range of either side of an estimate that is likely to contain the "true value" with a specific amount of certainty (depending on the size of the sample).

Contrived questions: Survey questions that are related to the subject being studied but are not necessary. This puts the respondent at ease or disguises the questionnaire's purpose.

Control group: The people, objects, or areas that are not subjected to the treatment of independent variables in order to maintain a point of reference.

Correlation analysis: A statistical analysis tool for quantifying the relationship or degree of association among variables, either bivariate or multivariate.

Counterbiasing questions: Stating questions in such a way that potentially embarrassing responses are either made to seem normal and common or are difficult to deny.

Cross-impact analysis: A method of forecasting technology in which one prediction is assumed to be true and to be the basis for other events.

Decision tree: An analysis tool that presents a diagram of a specific decision showing alternatives and outcomes.

Degree of uncertainty: The level of probability associated with the outcome of a decision.

Delphi method: A procedure for forecasting sales whereby a number of experts' predictions are collected and weighted, based on the experts' degrees of expertise. The combined forecast is returned and reforecasting is done until there is no added consensus.

Depth interview: A loosely structured interview in which the subjects are free to express themselves. It is aimed at uncovering predispositions and unconscious feelings and can involve more than one respondent in a group depth or focus group interview.

Descriptive research: Research focused on the accurate description of the variables in the model. A model is assumed to exist or at least has been suggested.

Dichotomous question: A question having a two-way response, such as "yes" or "no."

Discriminant analysis: The process of classifying objects or people into categories using predictor variables (e.g., product buyers vs. non-buyers by geographic locations).

Dispersion, measure of: Statistics that indicate how "spread-out" the data are. Standard deviation, variance, and range are commonly used.

Editing: The process of ensuring that all requested survey data are present, readable, and accurate.

Expected value: A decision-making technique that computes the probability and the payoff of an outcome. This is often used to determine the value of research information.

Experimental method: Testing hypotheses through the manipulation of variables and measuring the effect on other variables.

Exploratory research: Research aimed at discovering the general nature of the problem and the related variables.

Expost evaluation: Evaluation of the sales forecast values and the forecasting techniques. The evaluation of the forecast values should be approached on two bases: accuracy on an absolute basis and accuracy on a relative basis.

Factor analysis: The process of reducing a large number of variables into a small number of created variables or categories called *factors.*

Family life cycle: A list of stages in which individuals progress in life from single (living away from parents) to senior citizen II (sole survivor). Associated buying behavior and capabilities are analyzed for each stage.

Focus group interview (or Group depth interview): A loosely structured interview in which the subjects are free to express themselves, conducted by an interviewer with a group of respondents.

Frame error: Occurs when the list from which the sample is drawn is not the same as the actual population to be measured.

Graphic rating scales (also Continuous rating scale): A survey question technique in which the respondent places a mark on a line that may be numbered or labeled to indicate a comparative attitude rating.

Interrogation: Asking questions of respondents as opposed to observing their behavior.

Interval measurements: A scale in which responses can be ranked as greater or lesser by equal distances and which has an arbitrary zero point or middle.

Interview schedule: A list of questions used when interviewing respondents.

Itemized rating scales (also Specific category scales): A survey question technique in which the respondent selects one of a limited number of categories. For instance, the response categories might include "excellent," "very poor," and a few in between.

Judgment sample: A nonprobability sample design where the interviewers use their own discretion in choosing "typical" or "representative" informants.

Leading question: A question that suggests what the answer should be or indicates the researcher's point of view.

Level of significance: A statistical term that refers to the probability of rejecting the null hypothesis when it is true; known as *alpha* or Type I error.

Market potential: The industry sales that would result from the optimum development of the market.

Market segmentation: The process of dividing consumers into identifiable, accessible groups to which a different marketing program can feasibly be directed. Geographic location, size, or age might be characteristics in a market segment.

Marketing information audit: A marketing information audit is a systematic, critical, and impartial review and appraisal of the basic goals, objectives, policies, and assumptions underlying the information activity, as well as with the methods, procedures, personnel, and organizational structures used in the activity.

Marketing information system (MIS): An organized way of gathering and analyzing data on a continuous basis to help marketing managers make decisions.

Marketing research: Gathering and analyzing data to help solve marketing management's information needs.

Mean: The average of a set of terms, calculated by adding all terms and dividing by the number of terms.

Measurement: The process of assessing the characteristics of an object and/or their number, or the process of obtaining data that can be subjected to analysis.

Measurement error: The extent to which the research measures what is intended to be measured, or is valid or sound.

Measurement study: A research project that seeks to develop techniques to measure variables or attributes that are to be included in a model. An example is quantifying white-collar worker productivity.

Median: The value of the term that is larger than or equal to half of the other terms and equal to or smaller than the other half.

Mode: The value of the term that appears most frequently.

Morality: The loss or refusal to continue in the experiment of respondents from the various groups.

Multidimensional scaling: An analytical technique that identifies the dimensions upon which consumers perceive or evaluate phenomena (products, brands, or companies).

Multistage sampling (also known as Cluster sampling): A method of random selection in which the sample is chosen in a group rather than by individual sample elements. This term usually is used when geographic clusters of repetitively smaller sizes are used to select a sample.

Multivariate analysis: Any statistical analysis tool involving more than two variables.

Nominal measurement: A simple two-way or multiple classification scale in which numerical designations can be used only as labels and not for ranking purposes.

Nonparametric test: A statistical test that makes few assumptions about how the factor being measured is distributed in a population.

Nonprobability sampling: All methods in which units are not selected by chance procedures or with known probabilities of selection (nonrandom).

Nonresponse error: The difference between those who respond to a survey and those who do not respond. Higher response rates decrease the chances of such a difference.

Null hypothesis: The opposite of what a study is to prove. This is the hypothesis that is tested. If it is rejected, the alternative hypothesis is accepted.

Observation method: Gathering information by observing the behavior of customers or potential customers.

Opportunistic sample (or Convenience sample): A nonprobability sample design composed of individuals casually met or conveniently available.

Ordinal measurement (also known as Ranking): A scale in which one response is greater or lesser than another. Numbers are used to rank or order responses, as in the Likert scale.

Panel: Refers to a group of individuals who have agreed to provide information to a researcher over a period of time. Television viewing patterns or purchase patterns reported on a regular basis are examples.

Parameter: The factor that is to be measured in a population.

Parametric test: A statistical test that makes assumptions about the measured factor or parameter.

Perceptual maps: A diagram that shows the results of multidimensional scaling in pictorial form. It shows position, variables, and importance of variables in one diagram.

Population (or Universe): All the objects or people that possess a given characteristic to be measured.

Positioning: A strategy that involves placing a product or institution in the minds of consumers relative to other competitors.

Postcoding: The assignment of code values to responses after the responses are received.

Posttest: A project that involves measurement of dependent variables after manipulation of independent variables.

Precoding: Numbering response categories to structured questions prior to administering the questionnaire.

Predictive validity: The extent to which future attitudes and/or actions can be predicted based on knowledge of a given variable.

Pretest: A research project that involves measurement of dependent variables before any independent variables are manipulated to determine changes in the dependent variables as the result of changing an independent variable.

Primary data: Information gathered specifically to solve a current research inquiry.

Probability sampling: All methods in which units are selected by chance procedures or with known probabilities of selection (random).

Problem definition: The first step in the research design process. It involves determining precisely what the management problem or decision is and determining the information necessary to solve the problem.

Product life cycle: The stages through which all products and services go from beginning to end. It includes market introduction, market growth, market maturity, and sales decline. This analysis is often used in product technical and market research.

Quota sample: A nonprobability sample design in which the interviewer obtains a predetermined number of cases in each category.

Random error: Influences that bias the measurements in a nonsystematic manner.

Random sample: A technique for selecting members of a population in which all have an equal chance of being included (probability sampling).

Randomized response techniques: Gathering potentially embarrassing information by asking two yes/no questions, one sensitive and one harmless or meaningless. The respondent answers one of the questions based on a random determinate (e.g., a coin flip). Since the answer percentage of the harmless question is known, the embarrassing question response can be figured.

Ratio measurement: A scale that has a natural zero point or middle and equal distances between response categories.

Regression analysis: A statistical analysis tool for making predictions about one variable by use of known values of another variable.

Reliability: The extent to which the measurement results match reality, or the extent to which the process is free from random or variable errors.

Sample: Some part of a larger body specifically selected to represent the whole.

Sampling frame: A list of units from which the actual sample is drawn. Ideally, this is equal to the population.

Scale: A quantitative measuring device for a qualitative concept or attitude.

Seasonal index: A number or percentage for the period which, multiplied by the average value, results in a forecast that is adjusted for seasonal fluctuations.

Secondary data: Information that has already been published or collected.

Segment analysis: Analysis of sales and/or costs by products, territories, customer types, or channels of distribution.

Semantic differential: An attitude scaling device in which a subject is rated by how it compares to a list of bipolar adjectives (e.g., fast-slow, good-bad).

Sentence completion (also Story completion): An attitude survey technique where the respondent completes a sentence, much like an open-ended question.

Situation analysis: The analysis of information inside the firm and from published sources.

Standard deviation: A measure of dispersion of a set of numbers. It is calculated by squaring and summing the differences, dividing by the number of terms, and finding the square root.

Statistic: The value or characteristic of the sample:

Statistical inference: The drawing of conclusions about a large number of events (or the population) on the basis of observations of a portion of them (the sample).

Stratified random sample: A method of sampling that entails gathering data from different strata or levels. If the size of each subsample is based on the percentage of the total population in each strata, it is called a proportioned stratified random sample.

Survey method: Gathering information by asking people questions. Other methods include observation and experimentation.

Survey research: The systematic gathering of information from respondents for purposes of understanding and predicting some aspect of behavior.

Systematic error: Error that causes a constant bias in the measurements.

Systematic sample design: A method of selecting units from a list through the use of a selection interval (n) so that every nth unit on the list is selected following a random start.

t-Test (or Score): A statistical test of the relationship between a variable and one or more independent variables.

Tabulation: The posting or tallying of survey data into work sheets, computer punch cards, or terminals for statistical tests or other analysis.

Treatment: The combination of independent variables in an experiment that are introduced to certain units. Responses or dependent variables are measured to quantify a relationship.

Two-tailed test: A hypothesis-testing method in which the value of the true hypothesis in relation to the alternative hypothesis is not specified and thus is nondirectional. The name refers to the "tails" of a bell curve.

Universe (or Population): All of the objects or people that possess a given characteristic to be measured.

Validity: The extent to which the measurement process measures what it is intended to measure.

Variable: A value that is subject to change. This can also refer to data that are quantitative, as opposed to attribute or nonquantitative data.

Variance: A measure of the dispersion of a set of numbers. This is calculated by dividing the sum of the squares of the differences by the number of terms.

Word association (also Free or Successive Word association): An attitude survey technique in which the respondent gives the first words or thoughts that come to mind when presented with a word or phrase.

Z score: The number of standard deviations by which a particular term is above or below the mean.

Sample
Research Proposals

MARKET PENETRATION STUDY

FOR

PLANETARY-GEAR-SET-DRIVEN PRODUCTS

—United States—

Proposal Submitted to

Sherwood Winch Company

St. Louis, Missouri

May 1983

Note: Names, dates,
and locations have
been changed in this
sample proposal.

Background

Sherwood Winch Company is conducting the strategic planning necessary to evaluate opportunities within markets that have or will be developing a demand for planetary-gear-set-driven product lines. The specific purpose of this study is to identify the markets or market segments which currently are unserved or are marginally served <u>and</u> which provide the existing or potential demand for a new supplier of a specific planetary-gear-set-driven product line.

Strong growth in energy and mineral markets underpinned the success of the largest construction contractors in 1982. Construction firms in the U.S. alone reported the dollar sales for contracts signed in 1982 were 25 percent over the performance for 1981. The strongest growth was realized in the oil, gas, and energy related fields, with mining, marine, public works, and defense projects showing excellent growth potential for the near term. Because of intense competition from the continual introduction of new, more efficient lines of equipment from suppliers serving these markets, it is imperative to have the most accurate and timely feedback of the tempo, trends, and requirements of this dynamic marketplace. Greater demands being placed on the contractors, along with increased reliance on technology advances, make it necessary for the successful suppliers of the future to be the initiator and formulator of the needs of the marketplace, based on a clear understanding of emerging needs and trends.

Sherwood Winch Company has for some time been aware of the potential for gear sets that provide a greater efficiency and permit continuous duty usage. Central to the purpose of this study will be obtaining firsthand

112

knowledge from key user firms of the design characteristics required for known market usages of planetary-gear sets.

The goal of Sherwood Winch Company, therefore, is to set the pace with planetary-gear-driven products which industry now requires, but with which it is not presently adequately supplied.

Because of the importance of market data to strategic planning, it is necessary to prepare a reliable forecast of this fast evolving technology-oriented industry. The proposed study will concentrate on providing a comprehensive background of customer and competitor dynamics from which to evaluate future market penetration strategies for Sherwood Winch Company.

Scope and Methodology

To achieve the optimal results from the planetary-gear-products market penetration program, a two-phase study is recommended. Each phase would incorporate a different approach and methodology. This two-fold approach is designed to maximize the quality and depth of the results while minimizing the variable cost to Sherwood Winch Company.

Phase I results will be based on interviews with a select and carefully designed sample of decision makers from OEM's and end users. After identifying firms and decision makers whose viewpoints will provide a variety of perspectives on the planetary-gear products business, the first phase will feature open-ended discussions with these decision makers. These discussions will build on and be tailored toward the individual expertise of the person interviewed as well as his firm's perspective and sector of industry. This first phase then will serve to identify the market alterna-tives that might or could be expected for planetary-gear products usage and to determine agreement for the market trends expected by this select sample of decision makers. Phase I, therefore, will be qualitative in thrust and based on 40 personal interviews.

Phase II will be based on the foundation built in Phase I. Phase II, however, will sample a wide variety of OEM's and end users and potential end users to further explore market opportunities and quantify existing market dynamics for planetary product requirements. But more important, it would provide an important complement to and expand the perspective gained from Phase I in determining the trends to be expected in the future. By utilizing the appropriate statistical techniques, factors will be identified which underlie the pulse and direction of the marketplace as it now is, and which form the basis of the marketplace trends and marketing appeals which can be expected to emerge in the future. Phase II will be based on a carefully drawn sample of 300 interviews which will focus on each subsector of industry being examined. Phase II will result in the detailed analysis which will satisfy the study objectives of this market penetration program.

Planetary Products Market Penetration Program Study Objectives
The objectives of the market research to be done for the planetary-gear products market penetration program are suggested as follows:

I. Determine market size by number of units of planetary-gear-driven products for 1976–1986:
  A. Market Segments:
    1. Excavators:
        a. planetary swing (upper) drives
        b. crawler-track drives
    2. Log loaders and other logging equipment:
        a. planetary crawler-track drives
        b. swing (upper) drives
        c. planetary winches
        d. planetary-gear speed reducers for winch drives in lieu of complete winches.
    3. Mobile cranes:
        a. planetary-gear winches
        b. swing (upper) drives
        c. crawler-track drives
        d. speed reducers for winch drives in lieu of complete winches
    4. Truck cranes:
        a. planetary-gear winches
        b. planetary-gear (upper) swing drives
        c. speed reducers for winch drives in lieu of complete winches
    5. Pedestal cranes:
        a. planetary-gear winches
        b. swing (upper) drives
        c. speed reducers for winch drives in lieu of complete winches
    6. Compactors:
        a. planetary crawler-track drives
        b. swing (upper) drives
        c. planetary winches
    7. Blast hole drills:
        a. planetary crawler-track drives
        b. swing (upper) drives
        c. planetary winches
    8. Paving machines:
        a. planetary crawler-track drives
        b. speed reducers
    9. Offshore (jackup) drilling platforms:
        a. planetary speed reducers
        b. independent winches

10. Fishing boats:
    a. planetary winches
    b. speed reducers
11. Work boats:
    a. planetary winches
    b. speed reducers
B. Planetary product specifications (product sizes):
  1. Excavator swing (upper) drives and other speed reducers used in high shock applications: 3,500 ft. lbs. to 16,00 ft. lbs.:
    a. indicate top 4 to 5 categories
  2. Crane (upper) swing drives: 6,000 ft. lbs. to 24,000 ft. lbs. (non-high shock applications):
    a. top 4 to 5 categories
  3. Track drives ("propel boxes"): 7,000 ft. lbs. to 32,000 ft. lbs.
    a. top 4 to 5 categories
  4. Speed reducers: 6,000 ft. lbs. to 24,000 ft. lbs. (non-high shock applications):
    a. top 4 to 5 categories
  5. Determine design (safety) factor for each application

II. Determine major customers for each product category:
  A. Planetary-gear winches
  B. Planetary-gear speed reducers for winch drives and drives for offshore (jackup) platforms
  C. Planetary-gear (upper) swing drives on cranes
  D. Planetary-gear crawler-track drives

III. Identify major competitors and relative market share (to include self-manufacturers):
  A. For product categories:
    1. Planetary-gear winches
    2. Planetary-gear speed reducers for winch drives and drives for offshore (jackup) platforms
    3. Planetary-gear (upper) swing drives on cranes
    4. Planetary-gear crawler-track drives
  B. Determine strengths and weaknesses:
    1. Design
    2. Manufacturing
    3. Marketing
    4. Price
    5. Service
    6. Others

IV. Analysis of customer attitudes toward current suppliers and the possibility of a new source supply:
  A. Determine approaches used by current suppliers:
    1. Advertising
    2. Literature
    3. Personal sales calls
  B. Identify services offered by current suppliers
  C. Determine customer satisfaction with current sales approaches and services offered
  D. Measure market receptivity to a new supplier of planetary products:
    1. As a limited specialized product supplier
    2. As a broad scale product line supplier
V. Profitability analysis of major competitors:
  A. Product categories:
    1. Planetary-gear winches
    2. Planetary-gear speed reducers for winch drives
    3. Planetary-gear (upper) swing drives on cranes
    4. Planetary-gear crawler-track drives
  B. Measure cost and profitability data for 2 to 3 major suppliers in each product category:
    1. Major equipment lines
    2. Parts and service
VI. Determine importance of various customer purchase criteria for planetary-gear products:
  A. Product specifications:
    1. Life expectancy
    2. Physical size
    3. Duty cycle requirements
    4. Torque ratings required
    5. Weight requirements
    6. Design (safety) factors required
  B. Means of distribution:
    1. Direct
    2. Distributor
VII. Determine customer attitudes toward importance of product preferences, features, and appeals:
  A. By type of product:
    1. Price
    2. Lead time/availability
    3. Prior relationship with manufacturer

4. Proximity to distribution point
5. Warranty
6. After sales service
7. Spare parts availability
8. Design factors specified

VIII. Identify interaction of influence among decision makers involved in the selection of suppliers:
 A. Engineering
 B. Manufacturing
 C. Purchasing
 D. Operations
 E. Other

 IX. Recommended market penetration strategy for identified planetary-gear products:
 A. By identified market segments:
 1. Market targeting
 2. Market positioning

What is Expected of the Research Organization

In addition to satisfying the specific study objectives, Sherwood Winch management expects the Ruddick Research, Inc. project team to objectively evaluate the purchasing criteria used by those who buy and specify in decisions to select planetary-gear products within the markets being studied. In a sense, Ruddick Research, Inc. is expected to provide Sherwood Winch with an independent evaluation of how business is obtained in this industry, pricing structures, what customers think of the state of the art for planetary-gear products, and what steps Sherwood Winch might take to identify specific "niche markets" and move quickly into a competitive position within this growth-oriented industry.

Study Design Approach

In order to provide a multi-faceted "self-correcting" approach to this project, we propose to have two consultant teams working the problem simultaneously. The first team will build the data from the bottom up, based upon field interviews and widespread personal contacts. The second team will work from the top down, developing an industry model and profitability analysis of major planetary-gear suppliers which simulates industry activity and accounts for major input from secondary sources of information. The second team will also engage in a limited number of "special personal interviews" with knowledgeable industry contacts to verify competitive data on a macro-basis.

Corroborative Data

In addition to using the results of interviews for information on which to build our fact base, it is also proposed that an examination and analysis of other sources of data be made to give insight and broaden the scope of the study. For example, because of our experience in construction and petroleum industry markets, non-proprietary information, which we have already developed and which is contained within our files, will be used to strengthen the evaluation of these markets. Likewise, published reports and secondary sources of data will be used as background for the financial analysis of major suppliers of planetary-gear-set products.

The Report

Phase I will be presented in the form of a preliminary bound report. Phase II will also be compiled into a bound report. The Phase II report will consist of tables, a written analysis, an executive summary, and conclusions and recommendations. Phase II will be the comprehensive analysis which will satisfy the study objectives. A detailed index of tables and a table of contents will make the final volume a valuable reference tool.

Phase I is expected to take six to seven weeks to complete. Phase II will require an additional seven to nine weeks. We are currently in a position to begin work by early June.

Presentation

A personal presentation and discussion of each phase of the study will be made within ten days from time of notice of completion of each respective phase of the study.

Cost

Phase I of this study will require a budget of $24,400 for professional services. Direct expenses for this phase of the study, such as travel expenses, long distance telephone charges, and associated costs (i.e., computer costs, graphics, special reports, or directories required) will be invoiced in addition to the professional services charges. These are billed at our actual cost and are not expected to exceed $6,250.

Phase II of the study, to be initiated upon completion of Phase I, will require $29,300 for the professional services budget. Direct expenses, once again, will be billed additionally at our actual cost. Direct expenses for travel and communications for Phase II are not expected to exceed $8,450. Should savings in travel and communications expenses be found, our billing will reflect the smaller amount.

An invoice of twenty-five percent (25%) of the total professional services fees and direct expenses will be submitted ten days after work has begun on Phase I. Additionally, invoices for professional services fees and direct expenses to date will be sent monthly with the final invoice sent upon completion of Phase II of the report.

Policy of Ruddick Research, Inc.

Our background and experience qualify us to undertake the task as outlined. To protect your interests, we agree that any proprietary information Sherwood Winch may furnish us or that is developed during the course of this study will be safeguarded in accordance with our established professional standards.

We look forward with great interest to working with Sherwood Winch on this timely project. Our very best effort will be given to satisfying the study objectives contained herein. A signed copy of one of the enclosed proposals will constitute our authority to begin work.

RUDDICK RESEARCH, INC.

Morris E. Ruddick
President

Accepted by Sherwood Winch Company:

By: _____ Title: _____

Date: _____ Purchase Order Number: _____

PROPOSED EMPLOYEE COMMUNICATION
EVALUATION AND STRATEGY

Proposal Submitted to
Steveco Company of America
Belzu, California

October 1983

Background

The management of the Steveco Company of America, Belzu, is currently evaluating their formal methods of internal communication. The goal is to more effectively communicate programs, policies, and general information to their employees. In order to achieve this goal and be assured of a communication strategy that is both realistic and practical, it is essential that management have an accurate understanding of the attitudes and expectations of its employees. Without such information, the level of understanding and effectiveness achieved by traditional means of internal communication is left largely to chance.

It has been said that, regardless of the message or the channel of the message, communication rests most explicitly in the ears of the hearer. Peter Drucker states that downward communication, that is, communication from management to the work force, can work only after it has been informed and shaped by upward communication. In essence, downward communication is a response to the values, beliefs, and aspirations of those who are receiving the message. An understanding of these values, beliefs, and aspirations is necessary for downward communication to work effectively and for there to be shared understandings of reality and mutual goals.

The major challenge facing any organization, therefore, is to create a work environment where its people can contribute to the mutually understood goals of the corporation. Of necessity, this means the work force needs information—it needs feedback, as well as the personal flexibility and psychological support to interact, understand, and accomplish corporate goals as management defines them. This burden must be borne, not sim-

124

ply at the management level, but all the way down to the supervisory or foreman level, which must maintain relationships with their people that permit open and honest two-way communication on every issue of importance to the audience.

The understanding of these general principles is necessary to approaching and formulating an effective communication strategy at Belzu. General observations drawn from our Belzu plant tour and associated conversations were:

1. There are three distinct groups of employees at Belzu . . .

Group	Current Orientation	Affiliation
Headquarters Mgt.	Steveco	Steveco
Operations Mgt.	Job Function	Technicians
Hourly Employees	Self	Unions

2. The rotating shift of the hourly employees (an operational necessity) currently contributes to "organizational apathy." But it need not.

3. The employees have been losing their sense of belonging, corporate identity, and loyalty to a large, uncommunicative company that sacrifices their jobs to economics (fuel prices). Individuals feel they have no control over their destiny (job security) . . . regardless of whether or not they do a good job. Those who once prided themselves as being Steveco's finest have difficulty assimilating the loss of this distinction, not because of their work, but due to rising fuel costs. The unfortunate result is a weakening in morale which, over time, leads to organizational apathy, poor job attitudes, carelessness, and . . . accidents.

Although no single individual expressed the problem in these terms, it is our professional opinion that this underlies the root cause of Steveco's Belzu communication/accident problem.

To this end, an effective attitude survey program that provides for feedback and problem resolution is necessary in preparing a reliable and effective communication strategy. The basic purpose of the proposed study will be:

1. To study and evaluate internal communications and their effectiveness.
2. To identify and focus upon those methods that will increase and maintain the effectiveness of the safety program.

The implied needs, deduced from conversations with plant managers, are:

1. To recommend solutions to the personal and psychological distance between headquarters management, operational management, and the hourly employees.
2. To recommend a means of reducing the accident rate at the plant.
3. To revitalize an "esprit de corps," a sense of identity, pride, and purpose in being an employee of Steveco.

The specific objectives of this study then will be:

1. To make an evaluation of the effectiveness of Steveco's various channels of communication.
2. To determine employee attitudes toward management and supervisory level communication.
3. To measure employee perceptions of how well informed they are.
4. To determine employee awareness of management's goals and policies.
5. To measure awareness of specific aspects of the safety program.

6. To determine employee attitudes toward the importance of being a Steveco employee and contributing to the overall objectives set forth by management.
7. To identify factors related to motivational enhancement and job satisfaction.
8. To evaluate importance employees place on traditional communication tasks.
9. To identify existing informal patterns of communication.
10. To determine the communication strategy necessary to most effectively achieve management goals and enhance motivational enrichment.

The ultimate goals of this study then will be to provide effective and practical solutions to the communication and safety needs of Steveco, Belzu. Specifically, these goals will recommend an effective communication program that will have as its purpose the anticipation of problems and opportunities and the ability to effectively communicate company goals and policies in terms that will be understood by the employees. Additionally, they will identify the root causes of the current level of accidents and recommend changes to reduce accidents.

It is proposed that Steveco and Ruddick Research work cooperatively in the study in order to maximize the results and minimize the time and variable cost to Steveco.

Detailed Study Objectives

The objectives of the communication research study are to be as follows:

I. Preliminary Analysis (Phase I)
    A. Evaluate the effectiveness of Steveco's various channels of communication:

1. According to division.
    a. Chemical
    b. Refinery
    c. Smelting
    d. Other
2. According to job function.
    a. Management
    b. Superintendent
    c. Foreman
    d. Worker
    e. Other
3. According to the mode of communication.
    a. Oral
    b. Written
        1) Newsletter
        2) Bulletin Board
        3) Other

B. Determine employee attitudes toward management and supervisor-level communications:
    1. Determination of message importance.
    2. Reliability of communication channel.
    3. Importance of repetition to understanding and retention.
C. Measure employee perceptions of how well informed they are:
    1. For general company policy.
    2. For specific programs.
    3. For individual work groups.
    4. For adjoining work groups.
    5. For future welfare or benefits.

II. Detailed Analysis (Phase II)
    A. Determine employee awareness of management's goals and policies:
        1. General policies.
        2. Management's concerns toward the work force.
        3. Purpose of individual work units.
        4. Purpose of individual divisions.
        5. Function of Steveco, Belzu, as a part of Steveco corporate.
    B. Measure awareness level of specific aspects of the safety program:
        1. Reason for importance.
        2. Peer acceptance of program.
        3. Effectiveness of various communication tools to promote it.
        4. Individual areas of caution.

C. Determine employee attitudes toward importance of being a Steveco employee and contributing to overall objectives set forth by management:
   1. By division.
   2. By job function.
   3. By years employed by Steveco.
   4. By age.
   5. By race.
D. Identify factors related to motivational enhancement and job satisfaction:
   1. Security.
   2. Importance of job/craft.
   3. Relationships.
   4. Purpose.
   5. Environment.
   6. Importance of total picture/corporate goals.
E. Evaluate importance employees place on traditional communication tasks:
   1. To build morale and foster employee communication tasks.
   2. To keep employees informed and to avoid misinformation and rumors.
   3. To motivate employees toward greater productivity.
   4. To create an employee constituency that will support the company with legislators and on other.
   5. To reduce company turnover.
   6. To help avoid strikes and other labor unrest.
   7. To encourage employees to invest in the company.
F. Identify existing informal patterns and lines of communication:
   1. According to division.
   2. According to job functions.
G. Develop a demographic and psychographic profile of employees:
   1. Demographic
      a. Age
      b. Sex
      c. Marital status
      d. Number of children
      e. Number of years with Steveco
      f. Job functions
      g. Distance traveled to work.
   2. Psychographic factors
      a. Individual pursuits/interests
      b. Family interests

  c. Leader/follower

  d. Activist/inactive

  e. Pessimist/optimist

  f. Achievers/maintainers

  g. Traditional/trend conscious

 H. Determine communication strategy necessary to most effectively achieve management goals and enhance motivational enrichment:

  1. To improve communications.

  2. To improve morale.

  3. To build a sense of pride in being a Steveco employee.

  4. To reduce accidents.

  5. To maintain and improve productivity.

Planning the Study

The study shall consist of a two-phased effort. Phase I will be a preliminary investigation obtained by focus group interviews and a sampling of personal interviews. Phase II will consist of a major survey effort both in the plant and over the telephone at home which will provide the detailed, quantitative analysis from which an effective, practical communication strategy will be developed.

The preliminary phase will begin with four focus group sessions which will explore employee and supervisor attitudes and perceptions toward plant communication in general and the safety program in specific. A focus group involves an open discussion with 8–12 peers led by a trained group moderator (from our staff) who is adept at probing and guiding the discussion. The groups are exploratory in their purpose and are designed to elicit insights and concepts from which to design a much more strategic and meaningful survey questionnaire.

The focus group sessions will be closely followed by approximately 40 personal interviews. The personal interviews will provide input to refine the design of the survey analysis. They will, likewise, provide timely preliminary conclusions and recommendations. Phase I is expected to take approximately 4–6 weeks to complete.

Phase II of the study will be based on a sample of interviews with Stevecoans. The sample will be drawn in such a way that it will be representative of the entire work force from which it is drawn. A specific series of interview questions designed around the study objectives will be formulated. This structured questionnaire will have been pretested in the personal interviews to ensure that each survey interview obtains the optimum in information and each question is worded so that it is clearly understood. Each interview will be designed to take approximately 20 minutes to conduct. A total of 400 interviews will be made.

Tabulations and statistical analysis will be made at the completion of the interviewing to yield the optimum by way of interpretation of the significance of differences and relationships among the attitudes and other factors examined in the study. Phase II is expected to take an additional 8 weeks to complete.

Corroborative Data

In addition to using the results of interviews for information in which to build our fact base, it is also proposed that an examination and analysis of other sources of data be made to give insight and broaden the scope of the study. This will include secondary information and available reports by experts in this field.

Additionally, non-proprietary information which we have already developed, which is contained within our files, will be used to strengthen the evaluation.

Presentation

A personal presentation and discussion of each phase of the study will be made within 10 days from time of notice to completion of each respective phase of the study.

Cost

Phase I of this study will require a budget of $24,800 for professional services. Direct expenses for this phase of the study, such as travel expenses, long distance telephone charges, and associated costs (i.e., special equipment required) will be invoiced in addition to the professional service charges. These are billed at our actual cost and are not expected to exceed $6,500.

Phase II of the study, to be initiated upon completion of Phase I, will require $35,400 for the professional services budget. Direct expenses once again will be billed additionally at our actual cost. Direct expenses for travel and communications for Phase II are not expected to exceed $8,450. Should savings in travel and communications expenses be found, our billing will reflect the smaller amount. Invoices will be submitted monthly, beginning 10 days after work has begun, reflecting the professional service fees and direct expenses for that time period.

Survey Alternative

Should a lower budget alternative be desired, the methodology will be based on 300 survey interviews. The study objectives for this alternative would be as outlined in the preliminary analysis of the detailed study objectives. This study would, likewise, be presented in the form of a bound report with the personal presentation. The cost for this study would be $18,150 for professional service fees with direct expenses billed additionally. The time paramaters would involve approximately 8 weeks.

Policy of Ruddick Research, Inc.

Our background and experience help to qualify us to undertake the task as outlined. To protect your interests, we agree that any proprietary information Steveco may furnish us with or that is developed during the course of this study will be safeguarded in accordance with our established professional standards.

We look forward with great interest to working with Steveco on this timely project.

If this proposal is acceptable, please sign and return one of the attached copies indicating your approval to proceed. A signed copy of one of the enclosed proposals will constitute our authority to begin work.

RUDDICK RESEARCH, INC.

Morris E. Ruddick
President

Accepted by Steveco Company of America

By: _____

Title: _____

Purchase Order Number: _____

Study Option: _____

appendix B

Sources
of Secondary Data

CONSUMER DATA SOURCES

Guide to Consumer Markets. Published annually by Conference Board, this source provides data on the behavior of consumers, under the headings of population, employment, income, expenditures, production and distribution, and prices.

Historical Statistics of the United States from Colonial Times to 1957. This volume was prepared as a supplement to the *Statistical Abstract*. This source provides data on social, economic, and political aspects of life in the United States. It contains consistent definitions and thus eliminates incompatabilities of data in the *Statistical Abstracts* caused by dynamic changes over time.

Consumer Market and Magazine Report. Published annually by Daniel Starch, this source describes the household population of the United States with respect to a number of demographic variables and consumption statistics. The profiles are based on a large probability sample, and they give good consumer behavioral and socioeconomic characteristics.

Marketing Information Guide. Published monthly by the Department of Commerce, this source lists recently published studies and statistics that serve as useful sources of current information to marketing researchers.

Census of the Population. (Government Printing Office.) Taken every ten years, this source reports the population by geographic region, with detailed breakdowns according to demographic characteristics such as sex, marital status, age, education, race, income, and so on.

COMPETITIVE DATA SOURCES

Fortune Directory. Published annually by *Fortune* magazine, this source presents information on sales, assets, profits, invested capital, and employees for the 500 largest U.S. industrial corporations.

Middle Market Directory. Published annually by Dun and Bradstreet, this source lists companies with assets in the range of $500,000 to $999,999. The directory offers information on some 30,000 companies' officers, products, sales, and number of employees.

Million Dollar Directory. Published annually by Dun and Bradstreet, this source offers the same information as the *Middle Market Directory*, only for companies with assets over $1 million.

Thomas Register of American Manufacturers. Published annually by the Thomas Publishing Company, this source gives specific manufacturers of individual products, as well as the company's address, branch offices, and subsidiaries.

Moody's Manuals. This source list includes manuals entitled *Banks and Finance, Municipals and Governments, Public Utilities, Transportation*. These manuals contain balance sheet and income statements for various companies and government units.

Standard and Poor's Register of Corporations, Directors, and Executives. Published annually by Standard and Poor's, this source provides officers, sales, products, and number of employees for some 30,000 U.S. and Canadian corporations.

Almanac of Business and Industrial Financial Ratios. Published annually by Prentice-Hall, this source lists a number of businesses, sales, and certain operating ratios for several industries. The computations are from tax returns, supplied by the IRS, and the data allow comparison of a company's financial ratios with competitors of similar size.

Wall Street Journal Index. Published monthly, this source lists corporate news, alphabetically, by firm name, as it has occurred in the *Wall Street Journal*.

Moody's Manual of Investments. This source documents historical and operational data on selected firms and five years of their balance sheets, income accounts, and dividend records.

Directory of Intercorporate Ownership. Published in 1974 by Simon and Schuster, volume 1 contains parent companies, with divisions, subsidiaries, and American companies owned by foreign firms. Volume 2 provides an alphabetical listing of all the entries in volume 1.

Sheldon's Retail Directory of the United States and Canada. Published annually by Phelon, Sheldon and Marsar, this source supplies the largest chain, department, and specialty stores, by state and city, and by Canadian province and city. This source also includes merchandise managers and buyers.

State Manufacturing Directories. Published for each state, these sources give company addresses, products, officers, and so on, by geographic location.

Fortune Double 500 Directory. Published annually in the May-August issues of *Fortune* magazine, this source offers information on assets, sales, and profits of 1000 of the largest U.S. firms, fifty largest banks, life insurance companies, and retailing, transportation, utility, and financial companies. In addition, this source ranks foreign firms and banks.

Directory of Corporate Affiliations. Published annually by National Register Publishing Company, this source lists approximately 3000 parent companies and their 16,000 divisions, subsidiaries, and affiliates.

Moody's Industrial Manual. Published annually, this source provides information on selected companies' products and description, history, mergers and acquisitions record, principal plants and properties, and principal offices, as well as seven years of financial statements and statistical records.

Reference Book of Corporate Managements. Published annually by Dun and Bradstreet, this source gives a list of 2,400 companies and their 30,000 officers and directors.

MARKET DATA SOURCES

Bureau of Census Catalog. (Government Printing Office.) Published quarterly, this source is a comprehensive guide to Census Bureau publications. Publications include agriculture, foreign trade, governments, population, and the economic census.

Directory of Federal Statistics for Local Areas: A Guide to Sources. (Government Printing Office.) Published in 1966, this source looks at topics such as population, finance, income, and education from a local perspective.

Measuring Markets: A Guide to the Use of Federal and State Statistical Data. (Government Printing Office.) This publication lists federal and state publications covering population, income, employment, taxes, and sales. It is a useful starting point for the marketing researcher who is interested in locating secondary data.

Business Conditions Digest. (Government Printing Office.) Published monthly by the Department of Commerce, this source gives indications of business activity in table and chart form.

Economic Indicators. (Government Printing Office.) Published monthly by the Department of Commerce, this source gives current key indicators of general business conditions, such as GNP and personal consumption expenditures.

Federal Reserve Bulletin. (Federal Reserve System Board of Governors.) Published monthly, this publication offers financial data on interest rates, credit, savings, and banking activity; an index of industrial production; and finance and international trade statistics.

Monthly Labor Review. (Government Printing Office.) Published monthly by the Bureau of Labor Statistics, this source presents information on employment, earnings, and wholesale and retail prices.

Predicasts. (Cleveland, OH: Predicasts, Inc.) This abstract, published by Predicasts, gives forecasts and market data, condensed to one line, from business and financial publications, trade journals, and newspapers. It includes information on products, industries, and the economy, and it presents a consensus forecast through 1985 for each data series.

Statistical Abstract of the United States. (Government Printing Office.) Published annually by the Bureau of the Census, this source serves as a good initial reference for other secondary data sources. It includes data tables covering social, economic, industrial, political, and demographic subjects.

Survey of Current Business. (Government Printing Office.) From the Department of Commerce, this monthly publication presents indicators of general business, personal consumption expenditures, industry statistics, domestic trade, earnings and employment by industry, real estate activity, and so on.

County and City Data Book. (Government Printing Office.) This 1972 Census Bureau publication gives statistics on population, income, education, employment, housing, and retail and wholesale prices for various cities, SMSAs, and counties.

Sales Management Survey of Buying Power. Published annually by *Sales Management* magazine, this source provides information such as population, income, and retail sales, again broken down by state, county, and SMSA, for the United States and Canada.

Rand McNally Commercial Atlas and Marketing Guide. Published annually, this source contains marketing data and maps for some 100,000 cities and towns in the United States. It includes such things as population, auto registrations, basic trading areas, manufacturing, transportation, population, and related data.

Market Guide. Published annually by *Editor and Publisher* magazine, this source presents data on population, principal industries, transportation facilities, households, banks, and retail outlets for some 1,500 U.S. and Canadian newspaper markets.

Census of Population. (Government Printing Office.) Taken every ten years, this source reports the population by geographic region, with detailed breakdowns according to demographic characteristics such as sex, marital status, age, education, race, national origin, family size, employment, and income.

Census of Housing. (Government Printing Office.) Also published every ten years, this source provides information on types of structures, size, condition, occupancy, monthly rent, average value, and equipment contained, by city blocks.

Census of Business. (Government Printing Office.) Published every five years, this source supplies statistics on the retail, wholesale, and service trades. The census of service trade compiles information on receipts, legal form of organization, employment, and number of units by geographic area.

Census of Manufacturer. (Government Printing Office.) Published every five years, this source presents manufacturers by type of industry. It contains detailed industry and geographic statistics, such as the number of establishments, quantity of output, value added in manufacture, employment, wages, inventories, sales by customer class, and fuel, water, and energy consumption.

Business Cycle Developments. (Government Printing Office.) Published monthly, this Census Bureau source provides some seventy business activity indicators that give keys to general economic conditions.

County Business Patterns. (Government Printing Office.) Published annually, this source gives statistics on the number of businesses by type and their employment and payroll, broken down by county.

Commodity Yearbook. Published annually by the Commodity Research Bureau, this source supplies data on prices, production, exports, stocks, and so on, for one hundred commodities.

Handbook of Economic Statistics. Published annually by the Economics Statistics Bureau, this source presents current and historical statistics of U.S. industry, commerce, agriculture, and labor.

Market Guide. Published annually by *Editor and Publisher* magazine, this source lists data of 1,500 U.S. and Canadian cities. Data are compiled on population, principal industries, number of households, climate, and retail sales and outlets.

Economic Almanac. Published every two years by the National Industrial Conference Board, this source gives data on population, prices, communications, transportation, electric and gas consumption, construction, mining and manufacturing output, in the United States, Canada, and other selected world areas.

Directories of Federal Statistics for Local Areas and for States: Guide to Sources. (Government Printing Office.) These two directories list sources of federal statistics for local areas and for states. Data include such topics as population, health, education, income, and finance.

American Statistics Index: A Comprehensive Guide and Index to the Statistical Publications of the U.S. Government. Published monthly by the Congressional Information Service, this source indexes statistical publications of federal agencies, and it is a useful starting point for obtaining market data.

Business Statistics. Published biennially by the Department of Commerce, this source is a supplement to the *Survey of Current Business.* It provides information from some 2,500 statistical series, starting in 1939.

Standard and Poor's Trade and Securities Statistics. Published monthly, this source contains statistics on banking, production, labor, commodity prices, income, trade, securities, and so on.

Survey of Buying Power. Published annually by Sales Management Inc., this source gives information on population, income, and retail sales for each county and city of 10,000 population or greater, in the United States, Canada, and Mexico.

Market Analysis: A Handbook of Current Data Sources. Written by Nathalie Frank and published by Scarecrow Press, this book offers sources of secondary information broken down on the basis of indexes, abstracts, directories, and so on.

Business Periodicals Index. This source lists articles by subject heading from 150 or more business periodicals. It also suggests alternative key words that can be used to determine a standard of relevance in environmental analysis.

F and S Index. This detailed index on business-related subjects offers information about companies, industries, and products from numerous business-oriented newspapers, trade journals, financial publications, and special reports.

Reader's Guide to Periodical Literature. This index presents articles from magazines of a general nature, such as *U.S. News and World Report, Time, Newsweek,* and *Saturday Review.* It also suggests alternative key words that provide initial insight into the nature of the environment.

Statistics of Income. Published annually by the IRS, this source gives balance sheet and income statement statistics, prepared from federal income tax returns of corporations and broken down by major industry, asset size, and so on.

Public Affairs Information Service Bulletin (PAIS). Similar to the Business *Periodicals Index,* this source includes more foreign publications, and it includes many books, government publications, and nonperiodical publications.

Wall Street Journal Index. Published monthly, this source lists general news by subject.

Census of Retail Trade. (Government Printing Office.) Taken every five years, in years ending in 2 and 7, this source provides information on one hundred retail classifications arranged by SIC numbers. Statistics are compiled on number of establishments, total sales, sales by product line, size of firms, employment and payroll for states, SMSAs, counties, and cities of 2,500 or more population.

Census of Selected Service Industries. (Government Printing Office.) Taken every five years, in years ending in 2 and 7, this source compiles statistics on 150 or more service classifications. Information on the number of establishments, receipts, payrolls, and so on, is provided for various service organizations.

Census of Wholesale Trade. (Government Printing Office.) Taken every five years, in years ending in 2 and 7, this source provides statistics on 118 wholesale classifications. Information includes number of establishments, sales, personnel, payroll, and so on.

Census of Transportation. (Government Printing Office.) Taken every five years, in years ending in 2 and 7, this source presents three specific surveys: Truck Inventory and Use Survey, National Travel Survey, and Commodity Transportation Survey.

U.S. Industrial Outlook. (Government Printing Office.) Published annually, this source provides a detailed analysis of approximately 200 manufacturing and non-manufacturing industries. It contains information on recent developments, current trends, and a ten-year outlook for the industries. This source is useful in forecasting the specific marketing factors of a market analysis.

Merchandising. Published annually in the March issue of *Merchandising* magazine is the "Statistical and Marketing Report," which presents charts and tables of sales, shipments, product saturation and replacement, trade in and import/export figures for home electronics, major appliances, and housewares. Also appearing annually in the May issue is the "Statistical and Marketing Forecast." This gives manufacturers' sales projections for the coming year and is useful in forecasting certain market factors.

Standard and Poor's Industry Survey. Published annually, this source offers current surveys of industries and a monthly Trends and Projections section, useful in forecasting market factors.

Monthly Labor Review. Published monthly by the Bureau of Labor Statistics, this source compiles trends and information on employment, wages, weekly working hours, collective agreements, industrial accidents, and so on.

Ayer Directory of Publications. Published annually by Ayer Press, this source is a comprehensive listing of newspapers, magazines, and trade publications of the United States, by states, Canada, Bermuda, Republics of Panama and the Philippines, and the Bahamas.

COST DATA SOURCES

Moody's Investors Services. Published by Standard and Poor's this is a financial reporting source about many large firms.

Standard Corporation Records. Published by Standard and Poor's, this is a publication of financial reporting data of the larger firms.

Encyclopedia of Associations. Published by Gale Research Company, this source may acquaint a researcher with various associations for cost data pertaining to a desired industry.

Business Publication Rates and Data. Published by Standard Rate and Data Service, this index lists various trade publication sources.

Economic Census. (Government Printing Office.) This is a comprehensive and periodic canvass of the nation's industrial and business activities, taken by the Census Bureau every five years. In addition to providing the framework for forecasting and planning, these censuses provide weights and benchmarks for indexes of industrial production, productivity, and prices. Management uses these in economic or sales forecasting, and analyzing sales performance, allocating advertising budgets, locating plants, warehouses, and stores, and so on.

Trade Journals (Two examples shown below)

Food Service Trends. This is published by the National Restaurant Association. Wholesale Food Price Index and its percentage change is given for farm products, processed foods, and feeds as shown on page 10 of the June 1979 Food Service Trends publication of the National Restaurant Association.

Crest Report: (Chain Restaurant Eating Out Share Trends). Quarterly Supplement to Food Service Trends, published by the National Restaurant Association. Survey designed to tract expenditures and behavior in commercial segment of the food-service industry.

appendix C

Data
Collection Instruments

A SAMPLE MAIL QUESTIONNAIRE

A SAMPLE TELEPHONE QUESTIONNAIRE

A SAMPLE PERSONAL INTERVIEWING GUIDE

November 21, 1981

Dr. Reed Graham
Medical Plaza
2140 S. 78th E. Ave.
Tulsa, OK 74129

Dear Dr. Graham:

Marketing Research Associates is conducting a study in the Tulsa area concerning HOME NURSING CARE.

You have been chosen as one in a group of doctors selected to represent the physician sentiment in this area. Response to this questionnaire is completely voluntary, yet we hope you will choose to record your feelings on the short form enclosed.

This information will be used to help our client develop more effective nursing services.

Your response will be held in the strictest confidence. We are interested only in the collective responses of the physicians in this group. To help us achieve this goal, we ask that you please not put your name on the survey form or on the enclosed self-addressed return envelope.

We hope that you choose to help our client help you by taking a few moments to answer the enclosed questions.

Thank you.

Sincerely,

Robert E. Stevens, President
Marketing Research Associates

RES/mlr

Enclosures

HOME NURSING CARE QUESTIONNAIRE

Thank you for your cooperation. You can be sure that your responses will remain confidential. We are only interested in the total response trends of your selected group. Do not write your name on this form.

Please answer each question by placing an "X" in the appropriate space.

1. What is your specialty?

   A. _____ Internal Medicine   D. _____ Ophthalmology
   B. _____ Family Practice   E. _____ Urology
   C. _____ Surgery   F. _____ Cardiovascular and/
                                                   or Thoracic Surgery

2. How many years have you been in practice?

   A. _____ 0–10 years   C. _____ 21–30 years
   B. _____ 11–20 years   D. _____ over 30 years

3. What percentage of your patients do you estimate to be over 65 years of age?

   A. _____ 0–20%   D. _____ 61–80%
   B. _____ 21–40%   E. _____ over 80%
   C. _____ 41–60%

4. Where do most of your patients live?

   A. _____ north Tulsa   D. _____ west Tulsa
   B. _____ east Tulsa   E. _____ don't know
   C. _____ south Tulsa

5. Rate each factor according to the importance you place on it when selecting a nursing service for patient referral.
   Use the following scale and circle the number that best corresponds to your opinion.

1	2	3	4	5	6	7
very unimportant	unimportant	moderately unimportant	undecided or don't know	moderately important	important	very important

A.	Skill and training of nurses		1	2	3	4	5	6	7
B.	Nurses following physician's directions		1	2	3	4	5	6	7
C.	Feedback to physician of patient's condition		1	2	3	4	5	6	7
D.	Fees charged per visit		1	2	3	4	5	6	7
E.	Third-party reimbursement of nursing fees		1	2	3	4	5	6	7
S.	Availability during off hours (weekends, holidays, etc.)		1	2	3	4	5	6	7

6. Rate each of the following local nursing services in terms of how you believe it satisfies each factor.

Use the scale below and circle the number that best corresponds to your opinion.

1	2	3	4	5	6	7
very low	low	moderately low	undecided or don't know	moderately high	high	very high

A. Kimberly Nurses:

1.	Skill and training of nurses	1	2	3	4	5	6	7
2.	Nurses following physician's directions	1	2	3	4	5	6	7
3.	Feedback to physician of patient's condition	1	2	3	4	5	6	7
4.	Fees charged per visit	1	2	3	4	5	6	7
5.	Third-party reimbursement of nursing fees	1	2	3	4	5	6	7
6.	Availability during off hours (weekends, holidays, etc.)	1	2	3	4	5	6	7

B. Medical Personnel Pool:

1.	Skill and training of nurses	1	2	3	4	5	6	7
2.	Nurses following physician's directions	1	2	3	4	5	6	7
3.	Feedback to physician of patient's condition	1	2	3	4	5	6	7
4.	Fees charged per visit	1	2	3	4	5	6	7

1	2	3	4	5	6	7
very low	low	moderately low	undecided or don't know	moderately high	high	very high

5. Third-party reimbursement of nursing fees 1 2 3 4 5 6 7

6. Availability during off hours (weekends, holidays, etc.) 1 2 3 4 5 6 7

C. Tulsa County Public Health Nursing Service:

1. Skill and training of nurses 1 2 3 4 5 6 7
2. Nurses following physician's directions 1 2 3 4 5 6 7
3. Feedback to physician of patient's condition 1 2 3 4 5 6 7
4. Fees charged per visit 1 2 3 4 5 6 7
5. Third-party reimbursement of nursing fees 1 2 3 4 5 6 7
6. Availability during off hours (weekends, holidays, etc.) 1 2 3 4 5 6 7

D. Homemakers Upjohn:

1. Skill and training of nurses 1 2 3 4 5 6 7
2. Nurses following physician's directions 1 2 3 4 5 6 7
3. Feedback to physician of patient's condition 1 2 3 4 5 6 7
4. Fees charged per visit 1 2 3 4 5 6 7
5. Third-party reimbursement of nursing fees 1 2 3 4 5 6 7
6. Availability during off hours (weekends, holidays, etc.) 1 2 3 4 5 6 7

E. Pro-Med:

1. Skill and training of nurses 1 2 3 4 5 6 7
2. Nurses following physician's directions 1 2 3 4 5 6 7
3. Feedback to physician of patient's condition 1 2 3 4 5 6 7
4. Fees charged per visit 1 2 3 4 5 6 7
5. Third-party reimbursement of nursing fees 1 2 3 4 5 6 7
6. Availability during off hours (weekends, holidays, etc.) 1 2 3 4 5 6 7

1	2	3	4	5	6	7
very low	low	moderately low	undecided or don't know	moderately high	high	very high

F. Quality Care:

  1. Skill and training of nurses   1 2 3 4 5 6 7

  2. Nurses following physician's directions   1 2 3 4 5 6 7

  3. Feedback to physician of patient's condition   1 2 3 4 5 6 7

  4. Fees charged per visit   1 2 3 4 5 6 7

  5. Third-party reimbursement of nursing fees   1 2 3 4 5 6 7

  6. Availability during off hours (weekends, holidays, etc.)   1 2 3 4 5 6 7

7. Which nursing service would you probably use if you were going to refer a patient to a home nursing service? (Please rank in order of preference from 1 through 7.)

A. _____ Kimberly Nurses   E. _____ Pro-Med

B. _____ Medical Personnel Pool   F. _____ Quality Care

C. _____ Tulsa County Public Health Nursing Service   G. _____ Other (please specify: _____)

D. _____ Homemakers Upjohn

8. How frequently do patients request to be referred to a specific nursing service?

A. _____ never   D. _____ 41–60% of the time

B. _____ 1–20% of the time   E. _____ 61–80% of the time

C. _____ 21–40% of the time   F. _____ over 80% of the time

Thank you for your responses and assistance in making this study possible. Any additional comments you wish to make would be appreciated. Please feel free to use the space below to record them.

Health Insurance Survey

Hello, I'm _____ with Ruddick Research in Tulsa. With the
attention that has been given to health insurance across the nation in
recent months, we are conducting a statewide survey to learn more about
the differences among the types of health insurance policies available in
Texas. This is a bona fide survey and we are not selling anything. Your
answers will be confidential and used only to identify general trends within
the different areas of Texas. I'd like to chat for a few minutes with you
or the member of your household most familiar with your health insurance.

1. First of all, do you have any form of insurance to cover your medical
    needs?

    Yes (   )   No (   )   (If no, skip to question 5.)

2. (If yes.) Is it from a commercial insurance policy (from a private insur-
    ance company) and/or a government-sponsored program?

Government-Sponsored Program	(	)			
Medicare			(	)	
V.A., Military, Champus			(	)	
HEW, Medicaid, etc.			(	)	
F.E.P. (specify underwriter)			(	)	
Blue Cross					( )
Aetna					( )
Other _____					
(specify)					
Don't Know					( )
Commercial Insurance Policy	(	)			
Group					( ) ( )
Non-Group					( ) ( )

150

(If more than one policy.) Two policies with one employer ( )

   or   Two policies from different wage earners   ( )

(If neither group, non-group, HEW, or F.E.P., skip to question 5.)

3a. (For chief wage-earner's policy.) Which insurance company carries your health insurance policy?

Blue Cross/Blue Shield	( )
Aetna Life Insurance Company	( )
Travelers Insurance Company	( )
Prudential Insurance of America	( )
Connecticut General	( )
Mutual of Omaha	( )
Equitable Life Insurance	( )
Metropolitan Life Insurance	( )
Hartford Life Insurance Company	( )
Combined Insurance	( )
Lincoln National Life Insurance	( )
Provident Life Insurance Company	( )
Pilot Life Insurance Company	( )
CNA, Continental Assurance Company	( )
Washington National Insurance Company	( )
American Family Life Insurance Company	( )
Massachusetts Mutual Life	( )
John Hancock Mutual Life	( )
General American Life Insurance	( )
Bankers Life and Casualty	( )
American Fidelity Life	( )
Employer's Own	( )

Other _____

(specify)

Don't know	( )

3b. You said this policy is a group ( ); non-group ( ).

3c. (For group policy only.) Does your employer pay any part of the premium? (How much?)

All	( )

Three-quarters	(	)
Half	(	)
One-fourth	(	)
None	(	)
Yes, but refused/don't know how much	(	)
Refused/don't know	(	)

3d. Is this policy a single or a family coverage policy?

Single	(	)
Family	(	)

3e. I'm going to mention several benefits that different policies include. Please note which ones are included in your policy.

	Yes	No	Don't Know
Accidental Injury	( )	( )	( )
Hospitalization	(.)	( )	( )
Medical/Surgical	( )	( )	( )
Major Medical	( )	( )	( )
Student Health and Accident	( )	( )	( )
Dental	( )	( )	( )
Vision Care	( )	( )	( )
Audio Care	( )	( )	( )
Drug Rehabilitation	( )	( )	( )
Psychiatric Care	( )	( )	( )
Cancer	( )	( )	( )

3f. Now, I'd like to mention several factors and ask you to evaluate the company your policy is with. For each factor, respond with "excellent," "good," "could be improved," or "very bad." (Circle one for each factor.)

	Excellent	Good	Neutral/ OK	Could Be Improved	Very Bad
Service	5	4	3	2	1
Extent of Benefits	5	4	3	2	1
Prompt Payment of Claim	5	4	3	2	1
Cost of Premium	5	4	3	2	1

Friendliness of Agent	5	4	3	2	1
Overall Reputation	5	4	3	2	1
Ease of Filing Claim	5	4	3	2	1
Helpful Attitude of					
Policy Office Staff	5	4	3	2	1

(If only one commercial policy, then skip to question 5.)

4a. (For those with two commercial policies.) Which insurance company is your second health insurance policy with?

Blue Cross/Blue Shield	( )
Aetna Life Insurance Company	( )
Travelers Insurance Company	( )
Prudential Insurance of America	( )
Connecticut General	( )
Mutual of Omaha	( )
Equitable Life Insurance	( )
Metropolitan Life Insurance	( )
Hartford Life Insurance Company	( )
Combined Insurance	( )
Lincoln National Life Insurance	( )
Provident Life Insurance Company	( )
Pilot Life Insurance Company	( )
CNA, Continental Assurance Company	( )
Washington National Insurance Company	( )
American Family Life Insurance Company	( )
Massachusetts Mutual Life	( )
John Hancock Mutual Life	( )
General American Life Insurance	( )
Bankers Life and Casualty	( )
American Fidelity Life	( )
Employer's Own	( )
Other _____	
(specify)	
Don't know	( )

4b. You said this policy is a group (   ); non-group (   ).

4c. (For group policy only.) Does your employer pay any part
of the premium? (How much?)

All	( )
Three-quarters	( )
Half	( )
One-fourth	( )
None	( )
Yes, but refused/don't know how much	( )
Refused/don't know	( )

4d. Is this policy a single or a family coverage policy?

Single	( )
Family	( )

4e. I'm going to mention several benefits that different policies include.
Please note which ones are included in your policy.

	Yes	No	Don't Know
Accidental Injury	( )	( )	( )
Hospitalization	( )	( )	( )
Medical/Surgical	( )	( )	( )
Major Medical	( )	( )	( )
Student Health and Accident	( )	( )	( )
Dental	( )	( )	( )
Vision Care	( )	( )	( )
Audio Care	( )	( )	( )
Drug Rehabilitation	( )	( )	( )
Psychiatric Care	( )	( )	( )
Cancer	( )	( )	( )

4f. Now, I'd like to mention several factors and ask you to evaluate the
company your policy is with. For each factor, respond with "excellent," "good," "could be improved," or "very bad." (Circle one for each
factor.)

	Excellent	Good	Neutral/ OK	Could Be Improved	Very Bad
Service	5	4	3	2	1
Extent of Benefits	5	4	3	2	1

Prompt Payment of Claim	5	4	3	2	1
Cost of Premium	5	4	3	2	1
Friendliness of Agent	5	4	3	2	1
Overall Reputation	5	4	3	2	1
Ease of Filing Claim	5	4	3	2	1
Helpful Attitude of Policy Office Staff	5	4	3	2	1

5a. What kind of business does the chief wage earner in your family work for?

Agriculture, Fishing, Forestry	( )	_____
Mining, Oil/Gas	( )	_____
Construction	( )	_____
Manufacturing, Refining, Production	( )	_____
Transportation, Rail, Air, Water, Pipeline, Communication	( )	_____
Wholesale Trade	( )	_____
Retail Trade	( )	_____
Finance, Real Estate, Insurance	( )	_____
Services: Hotels, Auto Garages	( )	_____
Amusement Parks, Legal, Educational, Health, Social, Museums	( )	_____
Public Administration	( )	_____
Retired	( )	_____
Unemployed	( )	_____

5b. (If employed.) Approximately how many employees work at this location?

1	( )
2 — 4	( )
5 — 9	( )
10 — 24	( )
25 — 99	( )
100—249	( )
250—499	( )

500 or more　　　(　　)

Don't know　　　(　　)

5c. (If employed.) What town does the chief wage earner work in?
_____ What is the approximate population of that town?

10,000 or less　　(　　)

10,000–30,000　　(　　)

30,001–60,000　　(　　)

60,001 plus　　　(　　)

Don't know　　　(　　)

5d. (If employed.) How long has this wage earner worked for this employer?

Less than 6 months　　　　　　(　　)

6 months to 1 year　　　　　　(　　)

1 year (plus) to 3 years　　　　(　　)

3 years (plus) to 5 years　　　　(　　)

5 years (plus) to 10 years　　　(　　)

Over 10 years　　　　　　　　(　　)

6a. Are you married (　　)　　or single (　　)?

6b. Do you have any children at home or under your direct support (e.g., in college)?

No (　) 　Yes (　) 　(If yes.) 　How many? _____ (0–9)

6c. (If married.) How many wage earners are in your family?

None　　(　　)

1　　　(　　)

2　　　(　　)

6d. What is the approximate age category of the chief wage earner?

Under 20　　(　　)

20–24　　　(　　)

25–34　　　(　　)

35–44　　　(　　)

45–54　　　(　　)

55–64	(	)
64–74	(	)
75 plus	(	)
Refused	(	)

6e. Male (   )   Female (   )

7. Which of the health insurance companies in Texas have you learned the most about through print, newspaper, radio, or television advertising? (Limit to two and indicate first and second choice.)

Blue Cross/Blue Shield	(	)
Aetna Life Insurance Company	(	)
Travelers Insurance Company	(	)
Prudential Insurance of America	(	)
Connecticut General	(	)
Mutual of Omaha	(	)
Equitable Life Insurance	(	)
Metropolitan Life Insurance	(	)
Hartford Life Insurance Company	(	)
Combined Insurance	(	)
Lincoln National Life Insurance	(	)
Provident Life Insurance Company	(	)
Pilot Life Insurance Company	(	)
CNA, Continental Assurance Company	(	)
Washington National Insurance Company	(	)
American Family Life Insurance Company	(	)
Massachusetts Mutual Life	(	)
John Hancock Mutual Life	(	)
General American Life Insurance	(	)
Bankers Life and Casualty	(	)
American Fidelity Life	(	)
Employer's Own	(	)

Other _____
                              (specify)

Don't know   (   )

NAME _____ PHONE _____ CITY/TOWN _____

COUNTY _____ REGION _____ (1–5)

DATE/TIME _____ INTERVIEWER INITIALS _____

County Population:

10,000 or less	( )
10,001–30,000	( )
30,001–60,000	( )
60,001–100,000	( )
100,001 plus	( )

MOTEL STUDY
INTERVIEWING GUIDE

Date _____

Inn _____

Interviewer _____

Interview # _____

1. What is the purpose of your present trip?

2. How do you usually go about arranging for a room? (Probe for factors influencing development and use of strategy.)

3. Have you used the reservation services of other motel or hotel chains? How do you think the reservation services of this motel compare to the others you are familiar with?

4. Are there specific things you like or dislike about making reservations? What about this motel's reservation services?

5. Is there anything missing in present reservation services that you feel would be an improvement?

6. (If not volunteered in previous question.) How would you react to the idea of all reservations being made only by telephone?
   a. one number system
   b. physical evidence and personal contact

MOTEL STUDY

1. In which one of the following age categories do you belong?

Under 25 _____

26 to 34 _____

35 to 44 _____

45 to 54 _____

55 to 65 _____

Over 65 _____

2. Sex: Male_____   Female _____

3. What is your occupation?
    1. Professional-technical _____
    2. Top manager or owner _____
    3. Middle manager _____
    4. Sales _____
    5. Craftsman _____
    6. Operative _____
    7. Service _____
    8. Clerical _____
    9. Laborer _____
    10. Armed forces _____
    11. Miscellaneous _____
    12. Not in labor force _____

4. What type of company do you work for?
    1. Manufacturing _____
    2. Wholesaling or retailing _____
    3. Service _____
    4. Education _____
    5. Professional _____
    6. Government _____
    7. Other _____
    8. Retired _____

5. What is the highest level of education you have reached?
    1. Some grade school _____
    2. Completed eighth grade _____
    3. Some high school _____
    4. Graduate—high school _____
    5. Some college _____
    6. Graduate—four years college _____
    7. Graduate work _____

6. Which of the following categories most nearly approximates your annual family income?

1. $ 0–$ 4,999 _____
2.   5,000–   7,999 _____ .
3.   8,000– 10,999 _____
4. 11,000– 13,999 _____
5. 14,000– 16,999 _____
6. 17,000– and over _____

7. Approximately how many nights do you spend in motels or hotels each year? _____

appendix D

The Statistical
Side of Sampling

The sample size for a probability sample depends on the standard error of the mean, the precision desired from the estimate, and the desired degree of confidence associated with the estimate. The standard error of the mean measures sampling errors that arise from estimating a population from a sample instead of including all of the essential information in the population. The size of the standard error is the function of the standard deviation of the population values and the size of the sample. $(\sigma_{\overline{X}} = \sigma/\sqrt{n})$

$\sigma_{\overline{X}}$ = standard error

σ = standard deviation

n = sample size

The precision is the size of the plus-or-minus interval around the population parameter under consideration, and the degree of confidence is the percentage level of certainty that the true mean is within the plus-or-minus interval around the mean. Precision and confidence are interrelated and, within a given size sample, increasing one may be done only at the expense of the other. In other words, you may increase the degree of confidence or of precision, but not of both.

The main factors that have a direct influence on the size of the sample are:

1. *The desired degree of confidence associated with the estimate.* In other words, how confident does the researcher want to be in the results of the survey? If the researcher wants 100-percent confidence, he or she must take a census. The more confident a researcher wants to be, the larger the sample should be. This confidence is usually expressed in terms of 90, 95, or 99 percent.

2. *The size of the error the researcher is willing to accept.* This width of the interval relates to the precision desired from the estimate. The greater the precision, or rather the smaller the plus-or-minus fluctuation around the sample mean, the larger the sample requirement.

The basic formula for calculating sample size for variables* is derived from the formula for standard error:

$$\sigma_{\overline{X}} = \frac{\sigma}{\sqrt{n}}$$

$$n = \frac{\sigma^2}{\sigma_{\overline{X}}^2}$$

The unknowns in the $\sigma_{\overline{X}} = \sigma/\sqrt{n}$ formula are $\sigma_{\overline{X}}$ (standard error), σ (standard deviation), and n (sample size). In order to calculate the sample size, the researcher must:

1. Select the appropriate level of confidence.
2. Determine the width of the plus-or-minus interval that is acceptable and calculate standard error.
3. Estimate the variability (standard deviation) of the population based on a pilot study or previous experience of the researcher with the population.
4. Calculate sample size (solve for n).

For example, a researcher might choose the 95.5-percent confidence level as appropriate. Using the assumptions of the Central Limit Theorem (that means of samples drawn will be normally distributed around the population mean, etc.), the researcher will select a standard normal deviate from the following tables:

Level of Confidence	Z Value
68.3%	1.00
95.0	1.96
95.5	2.00
99.0	2.58
99.7	3.00

*Variables include such things as income, age, weight, and height.

This allows the researcher to calculate the $\sigma_{\bar{x}}$. If, for example, the precision width of the interval is selected at 40, the sampling error on either side of the mean must be 20. At the 95.5-percent level of confidence, Z = 2 and the confidence interval equals $\pm$ Z $\sigma_{\bar{x}}$. Then, the $\sigma_{\bar{x}}$ is equal to 10.

$$CL = \bar{X} \pm Z\sigma\bar{X} \qquad CI = \pm Z\sigma_{\bar{x}}$$

$$Z = 2 \text{ at } 95.5\% \text{ level}$$

$$2 \times \sigma_{\bar{x}} = 20$$

$$\sigma_{\bar{x}} = 10$$

$$CL = \text{Confidence limits}$$

$$CI = \text{Confidence interval}$$

Having calculated the standard error based on an appropriate level of confidence and desired interval width, we have two unknowns in the sample size formula left, namely sample size (n) and standard deviation (σ). The standard deviation of the sample must now be estimated. This can be done by either taking a small pilot sample and completing the standard deviation or it can be estimated on the knowledge and experience the researcher has of the population. If you estimate the standard deviation as 200, the sample size can be calculated.

$$\sigma_{\bar{X}} = \frac{\sigma}{\sqrt{n}}$$

$$n = \frac{\sigma^2}{\sigma_{\bar{X}}^2}$$

$$n = \frac{(200)^2}{(10)^2}$$

$$n = \frac{40,000}{100}$$

$$n = 400$$

The sample size required to give a standard error of 10 at a 95.5-percent level is computed to be 400. This assumes that assumptions concerning the variability of the population were correct.

Later tables in appendix D are provided to allow you, at several given confidence levels, to select the exact sampling size given an estimated standard deviation and a desired width of interval. Table D–2 gives the same 400 sample size as calculated here if an interval width of 40 and a standard deviation of 200 are desired.

Determining sample size for a question involving proportions* or

*Proportions involve such attributes as those who eat out/don't eat out, successes/failures, have checking accounts/don't have checking accounts.

attributes is very similar to the procedure followed for variables. The researcher must:

1. Select the appropriate level of confidence.
2. Determine the width of the plus-or-minus interval that is acceptable and calculate the standard error of the proportion ($\sigma_{\bar{p}}$).
3. Estimate the population proportion based on a pilot study or previous experience of the researcher with the population.
4. Calculate the sample size (solve for n).

The basic formula for calculating sample size for proportions or attributes is derived from the formula for standard error of the proportion:

$$\sigma_{\bar{p}} = \frac{p \cdot q}{n}$$

$s_{\bar{p}}$ = standard error of proportion

p = percent of successes

q = percent of nonsuccess $(1-p)$

Assume that management has specified that there be a 95.5-percent confidence level and that the error in estimating the population proportion not be greater than ± 5 percent (p ± 0.05). In other words, the width of the interval is 10 percent. A pilot study has shown that 40 percent of the population eats out over four times a week.

$$CI = \pm Z \sigma_{\bar{p}} \qquad\qquad \sigma_{\bar{p}} = \frac{0.05}{2}$$

$$\sigma_{\bar{p}} = \frac{CI}{2} \qquad\qquad \sigma_{\bar{p}} = 0.025$$

Substituting in:

$$\sigma_{\bar{p}} = \frac{p \cdot q}{n}$$

$$n = \frac{p \cdot q}{\sigma_{p}^{-2}}$$

$$n = \frac{.40 \cdot .60}{(0.025)^2}$$

$$n \doteq \frac{.24}{.000625}$$

$$n = 384$$

The sample size required to give a 95.5-percent confidence that the sample mean is within ± 5 percent of the population mean is 384.

The tables later in this appendix provide a simple method for selecting sample size at several alternative confidence levels given an estimated value of the proportion (p) and a desired confidence interval. Table D–5 gives the same sample size as calculated here if an interval width of 10 percent (± percent) and a population proportion of 40 percent are desired.

Since sample size is predicated on a specific attribute, variable, proportion, or parameter, a study with multiple objectives will require different sample sizes for the various objectives. Rarely is a study designed to determine a single variable or proportion. Consequently, to get the desired precision at the desired level of confidence for all variables, the larger sample size must be selected. In some cases, however, one single variable might require a sample size significantly larger than any other variable. In this case, it is wise to concentrate on the most critical variables and choose a sample size large enough to estimate them with the required precision and confidence.

Table D–1   Sampling Chart *Variables* (68.3% Level of Confidence, $Z = 1$)

Width of Interval	Estimated Values of σ									
	500	450	400	350	300	250	200	150	100	50
100	100	81	64	49	36	25	16	9	4	1
95	111	90	71	54	40	28	18	10	4	1
90	123	100	79	60	44	31	20	11	5	1
85	138	112	89	68	50	35	22	12	6	1
80	156	127	100	77	56	39	25	14	6	2
75	178	144	114	87	64	44	28	16	7	2
70	204	165	131	100	73	51	33	18	8	2
65	237	192	151	116	85	59	38	21	9	2
60	278	225	178	136	100	69	44	25	11	3
55	330	268	212	162	119	83	53	30	13	3
50	400	324	256	196	144	100	64	36	16	4
45	494	400	316	242	178	123	79	44	20	5
40	625	506	400	306	225	156	100	56	25	6
35	816	661	522	400	294	204	131	73	33	8
30	1,111	900	711	544	400	278	178	100	44	11
25	1,600	1,296	1,024	784	576	400	256	144	64	16
20	2,500	2,025	1,600	1,225	900	625	400	225	100	25
15	4,444	3,600	2,844	2,178	1,600	1,111	711	400	178	44
10	10,000	8,100	6,400	4,900	3,600	2,500	1,600	900	400	100
5	40,000	32,400	25,600	19,600	14,400	10,000	6,400	3,600	1,600	400

Table D–2   Sampling Chart *Variables* (95.5% Level of Confidence, Z = 2)

Width of Interval	*Estimated Values of σ*									
	500	450	400	350	300	250	200	150	100	50
100	400	324	256	196	144	100	64	36	16	4
95	443	359	284	217	160	111	71	40	18	4
90	494	400	316	242	178	123	79	44	20	5
85	554	448	354	271	199	138	89	50	22	6
80	625	506	400	306	225	156	100	56	25	6
75	711	576	455	348	256	178	114	64	28	7
70	816	661	522	400	294	204	131	73	33	8
65	947	767	606	464	341	237	151	85	38	9
60	1,111	900	711	544	400	278	178	100	44	11
55	1,322	1,071	846	648	476	331	212	119	53	13
50	1,600	1,296	1,024	784	576	400	256	144	64	16
45	1,975	1,600	1,264	968	711	494	316	178	79	20
40	2,500	2,025	1,600	1,225	900	625	400	225	100	25
35	3,309	2,645	2,090	1,600	1,176	816	522	294	131	33
30	4,444	3,600	2,844	2,178	1,600	1,111	711	400	178	44
25	6,400	5,184	4,096	3,136	2,304	1,600	1,024	576	256	64
20	10,000	8,100	6,400	4,900	3,600	2,500	1,600	900	400	100
15	17,781	14,403	11,380	8,713	6,401	4,445	2,845	1,600	711	178
10	40,000	32,400	25,600	19,600	14,400	10,000	6,400	3,600	1,600	400
5	160,256	129,808	102,564	78,526	57,692	40,064	25,641	14,423	6,410	1,603

Table D–3 Sampling Chart *Variables* (99.7% Level of Confidence, Z = 3)

Width of Interval	Estimated Values of σ									
	500	450	400	350	300	250	200	150	100	50
100	900	729	576	441	324	225	144	81	36	9
95	997	808	638	489	359	249	160	90	40	10
90	1,111	900	711	544	400	278	178	100	44	11
85	1,246	1,009	797	610	448	311	199	112	50	12
80	1,406	1,139	900	689	506	352	225	127	56	14
75	1,600	1,296	1,024	784	576	400	256	144	64	16
70	1,837	1,488	1,176	900	661	459	294	165	73	18
65	2,130	1,725	1,363	1,044	767	533	341	192	85	21
60	2,500	2,025	1,600	1,225	900	625	400	225	100	25
55	2,975	2,410	1,904	1,458	1,071	744	476	268	119	30
50	3,600	2,916	2,304	1,764	1,296	900	576	324	144	36
45	4,444	3,600	2,844	2,178	1,600	1,111	711	400	178	44
40	5,626	4,557	3,600	2,757	2,025	1,406	900	506	225	56
35	7,346	5,519	4,702	3,600	2,645	1,837	1,175	661	294	73
30	10,000	8,100	6,400	4,900	3,600	2,500	1,600	900	400	100
25	14,401	11,665	9,217	7,056	5,184	3,600	2,304	1,296	576	144
20	22,502	18,227	14,401	11,026	8,101	5,626	3,600	2,205	900	225
15	40,000	32,400	25,600	19,600	14,400	10,000	6,400	3,600	1,600	400
10	89,928	72,842	57,554	44,065	32,374	22,482	14,388	8,094	3,597	899
5	362,319	293,478	231,884	177,536	130,435	90,580	57,971	32,609	14,493	3,623

Table D–4 Sampling Chart *Attributes* (68.3% Level of Confidence, Z = 1)

Width of Interval	Estimated Value of P									
	50%	45%	40%	35%	30%	25%	20%	15%	10%	5%
14	51	51	49	46	43	38	33	26	18	10
12	69	69	67	63	58	52	44	35	25	13
10	100	99	96	91	84	75	64	51	36	19
9	123	122	119	112	104	93	79	63	44	23
8	156	155	150	142	131	117	100	80	56	30
7	204	202	196	186	171	153	131	104	73	39
6	278	275	267	253	233	208	178	142	100	53
5	400	396	384	364	336	300	256	204	144	76
4	625	619	600	569	525	469	400	319	225	119
3	1,111	1,100	1,067	1,011	933	833	711	567	400	211
2	2,500	2,475	2,400	2,275	2,100	1,875	1,600	1,275	900	475
1	10,000	9,900	9,600	9,100	8,400	7,500	6,400	5,100	3,600	1,900

Table D–5 Sampling Chart *Attributes* (95.5% Level of Confidence, Z = 2)

Width of Interval	*Estimated Value of P*									
	50%	45%	40%	35%	30%	25%	20%	15%	10%	5%
14	204	202	196	186	171	153	131	104	73	39
12	278	275	267	253	233	208	178	142	100	53
10	400	396	384	364	336	300	256	204	144	76
9	494	489	474	450	415	371	316	252	178	94
8	625	619	600	569	525	469	400	319	225	119
7	817	809	784	743	686	613	523	417	294	155
6	1,111	1,100	1,067	1,011	933	833	711	567	400	211
5	1,603	1,587	1,538	1,458	1,346	1,202	1,026	817	577	304
4	2,500	2,475	2,400	2,275	2,100	1,875	1,600	1,275	900	475
3	4,464	4,420	4,286	4,063	3,750	3,348	2,857	2,277	1,607	848
2	10,000	9,900	9,600	9,100	8,400	7,500	6,400	5,100	3,600	1,900
1	40,000	39,600	38,400	36,400	33,600	30,000	25,600	20,400	14,400	7,600

Table D–6 Sampling Chart *Attributes* (99.7% Level of Confidence, Z = 3)

Width of Interval	*Estimated Value of P*									
	50%	45%	40%	35%	30%	25%	20%	15%	10%	5%
14	460	455	441	418	386	345	294	234	165	87
12	625	619	600	569	525	469	400	319	225	119
10	899	890	863	818	755	674	576	459	324	171
9	1,111	1,100	1,067	1,011	933	833	711	567	400	211
8	1,404	1,390	1,348	1,278	1,180	1,053	899	716	506	267
7	1,838	1,820	1,765	1,673	1,544	1,379	1,176	938	662	349
6	2,500	2,475	2,400	2,275	2,100	1,875	1,600	1,275	900	475
5	3,623	3,587	3,478	3,297	3,043	2,717	2,319	1,848	1,304	688
4	5,682	5,625	5,455	5,170	4,773	4,261	3,636	2,898	2,045	1,080
3	10,000	9,900	9,600	9,100	8,400	7,500	6,400	5,100	3,600	1,900
2	22,727	22,500	21,818	20,826	19,091	17,045	14,545	11,591	8,182	4,318
1	89,286	88,393	85,714	81,250	75,000	66,964	57,143	45,536	32,143	16,964

appendix E

Sample Pilot Study

PILOT STUDY OF

CUSTOMER RESPONSE TO

BERRY'S FAST-SERVICE RESTAURANTS

—Kerrville, Maryland—

Prepared for

Bill Berry, President, Berry's Restaurant

Kerrville, Maryland

December 1983

TABLE OF CONTENTS

INTRODUCTION

Berry's Restaurant is conducting ongoing planning to evaluate how they might most effectively serve the Kerrville fast-service restaurant market. The current change in image, product mix, and name from "Bill's" to "Berry's" raises many questions related to the fine-tuning of the concept to "fit" the Kerrville market's expectations and responses to the initial "Berry's" opening. In order to be as responsible as possible to the customer base drawn by "Berry's," as well as to provide insight on decisions regarding the subsequent restaurant changeovers, an attitude study of "Berry's" customers was conducted.

This study, prepared by Ruddick Research, Inc. during December 1983, sought to:

1. Examine who the typical "Berry's" customer is;
2. Identify what their responses to "Berry's" were, and why;
3. Determine individual preferences relative to particular aspects of food items consumed; and
4. Evaluate customer responses to "Berry's" compared to major competitive fast-service restaurants.

The data for analysis were gathered in a two-step process. The first step involved in-store surveys. The in-store surveys were conducted from 6 A.M. on a Wednesday to 6 A.M. on a Thursday, and from 5 P.M. on a Friday to 5 P.M. on a Saturday. The total number of customers participating amounted to 1,542. The in-store and drive-through customer survey questionnaires asked for basic information on likes and dislikes but, more importantly, provided the names and phone numbers from which the next step, the telephone follow-up survey, was drawn.

It should be noted that the bias of the sample is drawn from those customers who were inclined to visit "Berry's" prior to any advertising. It is from this perspective that strengths are expected to be identified and capitalized on and weaknesses reduced. But the point should be made that opinions represented are those of customers who, for one reason or another, have chosen to dine at "Berry's" once or more, and not of the typical fast-service restaurant patron in Kerrville.

The follow-up telephone survey included 350 respondents. The size of the sample was ample in order to achieve a 90-percent confidence level in the answers. The responses from the 1,542 patrons surveyed in-store can be found in the appendix and compared with the same responses from the 350 drawn for the telephone survey sample.

CUSTOMER PROFILE

The most significant conclusions drawn from the analysis of "Berry's" customers is that "Berry's" is attracting a wide cross-section of the community demographically, and the overall impression of "Berry's" and the dining experience it offers is favorable.

Previous research of the entire Kerrville community conducted in May and June of 1982 revealed that almost half the population of Kerrville ate at fast-service restaurants twice a week or more and there was a growing concern and awareness of the healthiness and nutritional value associated with the foods Kerrville residents chose to eat. The response of the customers attracted to "Berry's" in its first weeks of opening reflected a positioning of the "Berry's" customer base focused on a crowd that eats out frequently and is nutrition-conscious. Some new "Berry's" customers indicated they never would have returned to a Bill's.

Roughly half (54 percent) of the "Berry's" customers surveyed dined at fast-service restaurants more than once a week. Actual responses to the question of how many times "Berry's" patrons had visited a fast-service restaurant during the last two months were as follows:

Number of visits (last 60 days)	Percentage of Berry's patrons
1	8%
2–4	19%
5–8	19%
9 or more	54%
	100%

More than three-fourths of the responses of "Berry's" customers to their dining experience at "Berry's" were positive. Responses in each of the rating categories were as follows:

Rating category	Percentage of Patrons' responses
Great	26%
Good	51%
Average	14%
Fair	6%
Poor	3%
	100%

Over 17 percent of those surveyed had visited "Berry's" previously and had returned because the experience was positive. More than 11 percent of the respondents visited "Berry's" because someone had told them about it. The inference is that the "Berry's" dining experience lends itself to building a repeat customer base and one that recommends it to their friends. This is a dramatic turnaround from the high percentage of Bill's customers surveyed earlier in 1982 who had visited once and said they would <u>never</u> return.

A total of 86 percent of the "Berry's" customers interviewed said they <u>would</u> return <u>and</u> order the same meal again. Only 10 percent said they would not repeat the order of the meal they had. Reasons were dislike of buns (2 percent) and high prices (3 percent). The others were undecided. Considering that 77 percent rated their experience as positive and 14 percent as average, it can be concluded that a good portion of those who rated their dining experience as average would not only return, but would return for the same meal.

There were some patrons who visited "Berry's" and were surprised to find it to be a fast-service restaurant. The sandwiches and salads in the signage gave them the impression of a sandwich shop.

Close to half (44 percent) of the "Berry's" customers surveyed visited "Berry's" for a noon meal, more than a fourth (27 percent) stopped in during the dinner hours, and 9 percent patronized "Berry's" during the breakfast hours.

Those Kerrville residents attracted to the first weeks of the first "Berry's" opening had a wide sampling of demographic characteristics. The predominant age group was the 25-to-34-year-olds (41 percent), followed by the 19-to-24-year-olds (27 percent). The 35-to-49-year age group comprised 17 percent of the clientele. Slightly over 39 percent were in the $17,000-to-$32,000 annual family income category (33 percent made less than $17,000 and 28 percent had incomes of more than $32,000). Nearly two-thirds were married. Almost 30 percent visited "Berry's" by themselves, while another 30 percent came with friends. Another 25 percent came with their spouses or dates and the remainder came with their families or relatives.

APPEAL DYNAMICS

An analysis was made that determined relationships between attitudes "Berry's" patrons were asked to comment on. Those who had a <u>positive dining experience</u> at "Berry's" were found to also have a very strong positive response to the tastiness of the food and the value for the money associated with the meal.

The outside sign and name of "Berry's" were seen to relate very strongly to the friendly atmosphere of "Berry's." The signage also shows a strong correlation with the decore. The "Berry's" name, in turn, also is tied significantly to the response to the sign as well as the friendliness of the servers. On the other hand, the name had an inverse correlation with the menu selection found available. But the outside signage does carry with it a message of warmth and trust associated with a nutritionally sound meal expectation, which, in turn is reinforced by friendly service.

The tastiness of the food is once again first related strongly to whether the dining experience is considered positive. The degree of tastiness associated with the meal eaten is reflected in the degree of strength given the rating of the dining experience. Menu selection was also related to the tastiness of the food. In other words, if the food was tasty and enjoyed, the menu selection was seen as favorable. Two other criteria were found very strongly related to the tastiness of the food. These were the healthiness and nutritional value of the meal, and the value for the money associated with the meal. What this means is that the stronger the positive response of the dining public is to the taste of their meal, the stronger will be their impression that the meal, in fact, was healthy and that they received a good value for their money.

The healthiness of the meal has already been seen to be positively correlated to the tastiness of the meal and the associated value for the money. What hasn't been noted is that the nutritional value of the meal is enhanced by the decor.

<u>Speed of service</u> was related significantly only to the friendliness of the servers. There was, however, a slight relationship noted between speed of service and the value of the meal for the money. In other words, a customer who was made to wait too long <u>might</u> not rate the value for his money quite as highly.

The <u>value for the money</u> associated with the meal is most strongly related to its tastiness and moderately with the health and nutritional value given the dining experience. The overall dining experience also has moderately significant relationships with the value for the money customers associate with the meal they had at "Berry's" <u>after</u> their dining experience. Friendliness showed a mild relationship to value for the money. The decor/atmosphere also was seen to enhance the value for the money of the dining experience. The decor also relates strongly to the nutritional value given the meal.

The actual opinions of the name "Berry's," the sign, the decor, tastiness, value for the money, and so on, came across overall as being very favorable. A strong rating of "good" went to all criteria except for value for the money, selections available on the menu, friendliness, and speed of service. The selection available on the menu did measure "good," but was only slightly out of the "average" category. The value for the money, likewise, measured "good," but was also on the weaker side of the scale compared to the other criteria. Friendliness fit in the "great" category, and speed of service measured just shy of being considered "great."

CUSTOMER LIKES AND DISLIKES

The in-store survey results revealed that when "Berry's" patrons were asked why they rated their dining experience as they did, the most frequent answers were that they liked the food and appreciated the fast service. This was followed by a number of comments on the nice atmosphere. These major comments were followed closely by a number of patrons who noted that they liked the salad and those who mentioned an awareness of the cleanliness of "Berry's."

When asked if there was anything else they especially liked about "Berry's," the in-store survey respondents reflected positive comments on the decor, the tastiness of the food, the free fruit, and the salad bar. These comments were followed closely in frequency by favorable mention of the friendliness of the employees, the fast service, the good french fries, and the wheat buns.

The in-store survey response to the question about areas in need of improvement or change was reflected by nearly 20 percent who mentioned the need for a larger dining area. This was followed in importance by a need for greater menu variety (6 percent), and a number of comments on high prices (3 percent).

The level of cooperation of drive-through customers in participating in the in-store survey was somewhat less than the eat-in and take-out patrons (due to time factors as well as time-of-day factors). Since this resulted in the sample being skewed somewhat toward the eat-in/take-out patrons on the telephone follow-up survey, a special focus was given to answers given by the drive-through customers on the in-store survey questions. It was found that approximately half of those who placed their orders at the drive-through windows had been to fast-service restaurants nine or more times in the last sixty days. Viewed slightly differently, this says that they eat at fast-service restaurants more than once weekly.

Drive-through patrons saw the pluses of "Berry's" as being related to the tastiness of the food, the fruit given away, the friendly and fast service, the salad bar, the french fries, and the 24-hour operation. The area mentioned most frequently by the drive-through customers as being in need of improvement was having breakfast served all day, followed by the prices being high.

The follow-up telephone survey asked what customers especially liked about "Berry's." The most frequently mentioned response (16 percent) was the fast service, followed closely by the pleasant atmosphere (11 percent) and decor (8 percent). The tastiness of the food (8 percent) and the salad bar (8 percent) were also mentioned by several, followed by a special liking for the chicken sandwich (7 percent). The friendly service, whole wheat buns, and the fruit were also recalled by several as the factors they especially liked about their visit to "Berry's."

The most frequent answer on the telephone survey to the question of what respondents would like to see improved or changed was nothing (39 percent). However, a desire for an expanded menu, as well as the mention that more sandwiches were expected (11 percent) from the implications of the sign, were also responses to this question. There were also several (6 percent) who noted the need for more dining space. Additional comments related to high prices and a desire for more variety in salad bar items.

The sample of respondents interviewed on the follow-up telephone survey revealed that over half (57 percent) felt the 24-hour operation to be important to them. A total of 41 percent said 24-hour service was not important to them and 2 percent had no opinion on the matter.

Only 13 percent of the nonbreakfast patrons recalled seeing what selections were on the breakfast menu (9 percent weren't sure). Many indicated they weren't even aware that "Berry's" offered breakfast despite having a menu with the breakfast positioned adjacent to the regular sandwiches. of those who were aware of the availability of breakfast, over half (53 percent) said the variety of breakfast sandwiches would prompt them to stop by and try "Berry's" for breakfast in the future, and 26 percent said it might prompt them.

FOOD PREFERENCES

Of the customers who ordered one of the burgers, the bacon-cheeseburger, or the chicken sandwich, over three-fourths (77 percent) indicated they preferred having the lettuce and tomato automatically put on the burger as an aid to fast service. They overwhelmingly liked the whole wheat bun (93 percent). A total of 78 percent said they liked the sauce, and 7 percent said they had no opinion on the sauce.

Fifty-eight percent of those customers who ate one of the hamburger/

cheeseburger selections at "Berry's" said they preferred fresh meat to frozen, and 42 percent said it really didn't matter to them. Only 33 percent said they were definitely able to tell the difference between the taste of fresh and frozen meat, and 18 percent said they weren't sure. One of the most significant factors mentioned relating to the positive dining experience had by "Berry's" patrons was the tastiness of the meal, however.

The bun was liked by 85 percent of those who ate the ham and cheese sandwich. The type and flavor of cheese on the sandwich was liked by all who had it. In similar fashion, the type and flavor of cheese on the cheeseburger was liked by 88 percent, with 2 percent indicating they really had no opinion.

The french fries with peels was liked by 82 percent of those who ordered fries. Half of those who ordered shakes said they would have liked a larger selection of flavors to choose from. (The sample only included 4 percent who ordered shakes, however.)

A total of 88 percent who ate breakfast at "Berry's" said they liked the breakfast sandwich they had. Three-fourths of this same group said they liked the bun. There were 38 percent who noted they would have liked a larger breakfast selection. Judging from suggestions (three made suggestions) of additions to the breakfast menu (pancakes, scrambled eggs, and hash browns), these customers were probably Bill's customers who no longer had these selections available to them.

Almost all who ate the salad bar (95 percent) liked it and none disliked it.

There were 5 percent who had no opinion. A total of 19 percent said the condiments offered were not adequate and made several suggestions for additions. The most frequently mentioned addition (25 percent) was for alfalfa sprouts. Other suggestions included cucumbers, cottage cheese, garbanzo beans, chick peas, bell peppers, fruit, and cauliflower. It was also suggested that a small salad be offered.

COMPETITION COMPARISONS

A total of 77 percent of the customers surveyed had been to McDonald's in the two months prior to being interviewed. Almost two-thirds (64 percent) had been to Wendy's, 53 percent to Arby's, 50 percent to Taco Grande, 34 percent to Bill's, and 27 percent to Burger King.

"Berry's" customers surveyed were asked to compare "Berry's" with other local fast-service restaurants on the criteria of delicious-tasting food, wholesome/nutritious food, and a good value for the money. Overall, the response to "Berry's" was quite favorable. Scores ranged from "Berry's" as very much better (5) to competition as very much better (1). When compared to Wendy's on delicious-tasting food, "Berry's" was perceived as somewhat better (3.51). "Berry's" also rated somewhat better (3.57) against Wendy's on wholesome/nutritious food. On good value for the money, "Berry's" and Wendy's were seen as being about equal (3.44). It should also be noted that a natural bias was expected from these answers. Respondents were first inclined to try "Berry's" (A Wendy's is only a mile away). Also, after having a favorable experience, the inclination would be skewed somewhat in favor of the last favorable dining experience, which, mostly likely in this case, was "Berry's." Therefore, the interpretation was made quite stringently in order not to inflate the evaluation of "Berry's" competitive edge.

"Berry's" was seen as being somewhat better than Arby's on tastiness (3.64), nutritious food (3.62), and good value for the money (3.76). "Berry's" was also seen as being somewhat better overall than McDonald's on tastiness (4.16) and wholesone food (4.24), but with much greater strength. "Berry's" was perceived overall as being equal (3.30) to McDonald's on value for the money.

"Berry's" was rated as somewhat better than Burger King on tastiness (4.12), wholesomeness of food (4.14), and good value for the money (3.83). When compared to Bill's in Kerrville, "Berry's" was felt to be equal in tastiness (3.27), somewhat better in wholesomeness (4.25) and in value (3.81).

The factors most highly correlated with the tendency of customers to rate "Berry's" as better than Wendy's, Arby's, McDonalds, Burger King, or Bill's was the tastiness of the meat and the nutritional value associated with the meal eaten. In other words, the stronger the positive response of the customer to the tastiness and nutritional wholesomeness of a meal enjoyed at "Berry's," the stronger will be the tendency for "Berry's" to retain the competitive edge in the minds of customers.

As a final comparison, customers surveyed were asked to imagine they were late in getting around to eating a meal. They were told to assume that they had decided to go to a fast-service restaurant and that they were <u>very hungry</u>. They were asked to assume the locations were close between a "Berry's" and Wendy's. The question was, which would be their choice? A total of 68 percent said they would choose "Berry's." Reasons included because they liked the food better, they liked the salad, they preferred the "Berry's" chicken sandwich, they preferred the variety, and they liked the fast service. Those who chose Wendy's did so because of price for children's items, preference for Wendy's burgers, and the availability of chili.

The same situation was posed between "Berry's" and Bill's. "Berry's" was chosen by 89 percent of those interviewed. Reasons given included that they liked the food better, they liked the tastiness of the food, they liked the salad, or they wouldn't go to Bill's.

CONCLUSIONS AND RECOMMENDATIONS

Conclusions from the Kerrville-wide market study conducted in April and May of 1982 are summarized as follows:

1. Kerrville residents eat at fast-food restaurants quite frequently. The frequency is expected to increase among those who eat at fast-service restaurants once or more weekly.

2. The trend toward breakfast eaten at a fast-food restaurant is expected to grow.

3. An awareness and concern over the healthiness of foods eaten is emerging in the Kerrville market. Adults concerned with their own health as well as their children's health will respond to foods that are higher in nutritional value <u>and</u> also taste good.

4. Bill's in Kerrville in April and May of 1982 suffered from a poor image and low market share due to major factors such as a dislike for the taste of the burgers, slow service, and an image that sought the children crowd, but which had nothing special for the children once it was tried.

5. Almost half of the fast-service restaurant visits originate from the home; nearly 20 percent originate from the place of work. A convenience to save time was the most frequently mentioned motivation for visiting a fast-food restaurant, followed by a break from cooking and the need to enjoy a particular food item. The desire to eat a particular food item was also the primary reason for visiting the fast-service restaurant patrons went to most frequently.

6. Taste was mentioned as the most important factor when choosing one fast-food chain over another. This was followed by convenience of the location, fast service, availability of the favorite menu item, price, nutritional value of the food, and the availability of a salad bar.

Recommendations from the April/May study were to adopt:

1. A wider variety in the menu, to include:
   Salad bar
   Ham and cheese sandwich
   Barbecue chicken
   Chicken sandwich
   Fresh fruit dessert

2. An easy-to-scan menu where item categories could be easily identified.

3. A well-coordinated multimedia advertising campaign that stressed a wider menu selection; inclusion of a salad bar; tasty, fresh, quality food; nutritionally sound meals; and fast, friendly service. It was noted that a "nutritionally balanced, convenient, family-oriented meal for the discriminating tastes of active adults" would engender a great deal of appeal to a wide cross-section of the community.

4. A secondary focus on the breakfast market.

Conclusions from the survey of "Berry's" customers in December of 1983 revealed the following:

1. "Berry's" has been drawing upon a much wider cross-section of the community demographically than was Bill's earlier this year. Likewise, the response to "Berry's" has been quite favorable.

2. "Berry's" customers dine at fast-food restaurants frequently and place importance on the nutritional aspects of the food they eat.

3. It was seen that "Berry's" customers are willing to pay for quality, wholesomeness, tastiness, fast service, and pleasant surroundings. Prices are currently seen as a good value for the money by most of the market being penetrated. This can be maintained if the high levels of tastiness, speed, and friendliness are maintained. An exception to the response to pricing would be from some who brought children and viewed the cost of the meal as expensive for a "family" meal.

4. Many "Berry's" customers were expecting something other than a fast-service restaurant based on conclusions they drew from the name and the sign, which says sandwiches and salads. Once the meal was experienced, the overall impression was generally good. However, slight modifications in the menu selection could cause further reinforcement and market penetration.

5. Several "Berry's" patrons were expecting breakfast meals at other than breakfast hours. A single breakfast sandwich served at all times (and compatible with the other mealtime product mix) would serve to expand the sandwich concept and provide further penetration into the late-evening/night-shift market.

6. The friendliness and fast service come across very well at

"Berry's." These criteria, when combined with a nutritional, tasty meal in a pleasant atmosphere, result in the conclusion by the customer that the dining experience was a good value for the money.

7. There is a weakness in the awareness of breakfast being offered at "Berry's" despite the proximity of the breakfast items to the sandwich/burger offerings on the menu.

8. "Berry's" customers also visit Wendy's, Arby's, and McDonald's frequently. "Berry's" is evaluated by customers as somewhat better overall than its major competitors, which would be Wendy's, followed by Arby's. It is viewed as close to being very much better than McDonald's in taste and nutritional value. "Berry's" is perceived as equal to Arby's and McDonald's in value for the money.

9. Tastiness, the nutritional value of the meal, and value for the money at "Berry's" were found to be very highly correlated with the tendency to rate "Berry's" as better than their major competition.

10. The spread of distance from home and work of the patrons who visited the first "Berry's" indicates that other Bill's locations to be converted should expect a similar favorable response, with variance allowed for the demographic peculiarites of the individual locations.

11. There were no significant problems in response to the new buns, the cheeses, the sauce used on the burgers, or the new larger french fries. There was some comment expressing a need for more flavor selection for the fruit, shakes, and the need for adding certain condiments to the salad bar.

Recommendations for future "Berry's" openings would include the following:

1. A wider variety in the menu selection, to include:
    Egg and bacon sandwich with lettuce and tomato (24-hour)
    Egg sandwich with lettuce and tomato (24-hour)
    Bacon, lettuce, and tomato sandwich
    Cold sandwich selection
    Roast beef sandwich
    A smaller salad to go with sandwiches

2. A well-coordinated multimedia advertising campaign that would focus on:

> The small specialty restaurant image
> Nutritionally balanced meals
> Wholesome, fresh, tasty, quality foods
> Fast, friendly service
> Wider menu selection
> Individual favorite food item
> Salad bar
> 24-hour drive-through service
> Breakfast sandwiches
> Hot, nutritious, light dinner sandwiches.

3. The introduction of "Berry's" to Kerrville should maintain as low a profile as possible to "previously being a Bill's."

BERRY'S TELEPHONE SURVEY RESULTS*

Berry's Dining Experience Rating

Rating	Percentage
Great	26%
Good	51
Average	14
Fair	6
Poor	3
TOTAL	100%

Number of Fast-Service Visits in Last Two Months

Number of Visits	Percentage
1	7%
2–4	19
5–8	19
9 or more	55
TOTAL	100%

*Sample size of 350.

Reason for Visiting "Berry's"

Reason	Percentage
Driving by	47%
Live close by	15
Heard about it	11
Visited before	17
With someone	4
Close to work	4
To try it	2
TOTAL	100%

Respondent's Sex

Category	Percentage
Male	51%
Female	49
TOTAL	100%

Respondent's Age (Years)

Category	Percentage
Under 18	9%
18–24	27
25–34	41
35–49	17
50 or above	6
TOTAL	100%

Type of Visit

Type	Percentage
Take-out	13%
Eat-in	76
Drive-through	11
TOTAL	100%

Time of Day of Visit

Time	Percentage
5:30 A.M.–10:30 A.M.	8%
10:31 A.M.– 2:00 P.M.	46
2:01 P.M.– 5:00 P.M.	19

5:01 P.M.–10:00 P.M.	26
10:01 P.M.– 5:30 A.M.	1
TOTAL	100%

Day of Visit

Category	Percentage
Weekday	55%
Weekend	45
TOTAL	100%

Opinion of the Name "Berry's"

Rating	Percentage
Great	17%
Good	73
In-between	4
Don't think highly of	4
Poor	0
Don't know/no opinion	2
TOTAL	100%

Opinion of "Berry's" Outside Signs

Rating	Percentage
Great	26%
Good	63
In-between	3
Don't think highly of	1
Poor	1
Don't know/no opinion	13
TOTAL	100%

Opinion of "Berry's" Menu Selection

Rating	Percentage
Great	10%
Good	63
In-between	11
Don't think highly of	10
Poor	3
Don't know/no opinion	3
TOTAL	100%

Opinion of Tastiness of Meal at "Berry's"

Rating	Percentage
Great	31%
Good	54
In-between	5
Don't think highly of	6
Poor	2
Don't know/no opinion	2
TOTAL	100%

Opinion of Healthiness and Nutritional Value of "Berry's" Meal

Rating	Percentage
Great	24%
Good	57
In-between	4
Don't think highly of	1
Poor	2
Don't know/no opinion	12
TOTAL	100%

Opinion of Speed of "Berry's" Service

Rating	Percentage
Great	48%
Good	46
In-between	3
Don't think highly of	2
Poor	1
Don't know/no opinion	0
TOTAL	100%

Opinion of Friendliness of "Berry's" Service

Rating	Percentage
Great	53%
Good	42
In-between	2
Don't think highly of	1
Poor	0
Don't know/no opinion	2
TOTAL	100%

Opinion of the Value of Your Meal for the Money at "Berry's"

Rating	Percentage
Great	19%
Good	62
In-between	7
Don't think highly of	7
Poor	3
Don't know/no opinion	2
TOTAL	100%

Have You Visited McDonald's in the Last Two Months?

	Percentage
Visited	77%
Not visited	23
TOTAL	100%

Have You Visited Wendy's in the Last Two Months?

	Percentage
Visited	64%
Not visited	36
TOTAL	100%

Have You Visited Burger King in the Last Two Months?

	Percentage
Visited	27%
Not visited	73
TOTAL	100%

Have You Visited Arby's in the Last Two Months

	Percentage
Visited	53%
Not visited	47
TOTAL	100%

"Berry's" to Wendy's Comparison

Comparing On:	"Berry's" Very Much Better	"Berry's" Somewhat Better	They Are Both Equal	Wendy's Somewhat Better	Wendy's Very Much Better	Don't Know	Total
Delicious-Tasting Food	21%	24%	31%	13%	3%	8%	100%
Wholesome, Nutritious Food	18%	23%	43%	2%	3%	11%	100%
Good Value for Money	20%	23%	35%	10%	6%	6%	100%

"Berry's" to Arby's Comparison

Comparing On:	"Berry's" Very Much Better	"Berry's" Somewhat Better	They Are Both Equal	Arby's Somewhat Better	Arby's Very Much Better	Don't Know	Total
Delicious-Tasting Food	25%	24%	24%	12%	3%	12%	100%
Wholesome, Nutritious Food	22%	22%	37%	5%	3%	11%	100%
Good Value for Money	24%	25%	36%	5%	–%	10%	100%

"Berry's" to McDonald's Comparison

Comparing On:	"Berry's" Very Much Better	"Berry's" Somewhat Better	They Are Both Equal	McDonald's Somewhat Better	McDonald's Very Much Better	Don't Know	Total
Delicious-Tasting Food	45%	25%	13%	7%	1%	9%	100%
Wholesome, Nutritious Food	42%	30%	17%	–%	1%	10%	100%
Good Value for Money	20%	17%	33%	15%	7%	8%	100%

"Berry's" to Burger King Comparison

Comparing On:	"Berry's" Very Much Better	"Berry's" Somewhat Better	They Are Both Equal	Burger King Somewhat Better	Burger King Very Much Better	Don't Know	Total
Delicious-Tasting Food	33%	25%	9%	6%	1%	26%	100%
Wholesome, Nutritious Food	32%	19%	22%	–%	–%	27%	100%
Good Value for Money	23%	24%	23%	5%	1%	24%	100%

"Berry's" to Bill's Comparison

Comparing On:	"Berry's" Very Much Better	"Berry's" Somewhat Better	They Are Both Equal	Bill's Somewhat Better	Bill's Very Much Better	Don't Know	Total
Delicious-Tasting Food	40%	21%	12%	12%	3%	1%	100%
Wholesome, Nutritious Food	38%	21%	17%	1%	–%	23%	100%
Good Value for Money	26%	16%	30%	4%	1%	23%	100%

Have You Visited Taco Grande in the Last Two Months?

	Percentage
Visited	50%
Not visited	50
TOTAL	100%

Have You Visited Bill's in the Last Two Months?

	Percentage
Visited	34%
Not visited	66
TOTAL	100%

Will You Order the Same Meal at "Berry's" Again?

	Percentage
Yes	86%
No	10
Maybe	1
Don't know	3
TOTAL	100%

(If Ordered Burger, Bacon Cheeseburger, or Chicken Sandwich)

Do You Prefer Lettuce and Tomato Already on Sandwich?

	Percentage
Yes	77%
No	23
No opinion	0
TOTAL	100%

Did You Like the Bun?

	Percentage
Yes	93%
No	7
No opinion	0
TOTAL	100%

Did You Like the Sauce?

	Percentage
Yes	78%
No	15
No opinion	7
TOTAL	100%

(If Ordered Burger Only)

Do You Prefer Fresh or Frozen Meat?

Preference	Percentage
Fresh meat	58%
Doesn't matter	42
TOTAL	100%

Could You Tell Burger Had Fresh Meat?

	Percentage
Yes	33%
No	49
Not sure	18
TOTAL	100%

(For Ham and Cheese Only)

Did You Like the Bun?

	Percentage
Yes	85%
No	15
No opinion	0
TOTAL	100%

Did You Like the Type and Flavor of Cheese?

	Percentage
Yes	100%
No	0
No opinion	0
TOTAL	100%

(For Cheeseburgers and Bacon Cheeseburgers Only)

Did You Like the Type and Flavor of Cheese?

	Percentage
Yes	87%
No	10
No opinion	3
TOTAL	100%

(For French Fries Only)

Did You Like the Thicker Fries with Peels?

	Percentage
Yes	82%
No	18
No opinion	0
TOTAL	100%

(For Shakes Only)

Was the Selection of Shakes Sufficient?

	Percentage
Yes	50%
No	50
No opinion	0
TOTAL	100%

(For Breakfast Sandwich Only)

Did You Like the Breakfast Sandwich Selection?

	Percentage
Yes	88%
No	12
No opinion	0
TOTAL	100%

Did You Like the Bun?

	Percentage
Yes	75%
No	25
No opinion	0
TOTAL	100%

Would You Prefer a Larger Breakfast Selection?

	Percentage
Yes	38%
No	62
No opinion	0
TOTAL	100%

(For Salad Bar Only)

Did You Like the Salad You Had?

	Percentage
Yes	95%
No	0
No opinion	5
TOTAL	100%

Was the Selection of Condiments Adequate?

	Percentage
Yes	76%
No	19
No opinion	5
TOTAL	100%

(For Other Than Breakfast Patrons)

Do YoU Recall Selections Available on Breakfast Menu?

	Percentage
Yes	13%
No	78
Not sure	9
TOTAL	100%

(For "Yes" and "Not Sure" Above)

Will the Breakfast Variety Prompt You to Stop By for It?

	Percentage
Yes	53%
No	21
No opinion	26
TOTAL	100%

How Important Is the 24-Hour Service?

	Percentage
Very important	31%
Somewhat important	26
In-between	0
Not very important	22
Not important at all	19
Don't know/no opinion	2
TOTAL	100%

On Your Visit to "Berry's," Were You Alone or with Someone?

	Percentage
Alone	29%
With friends	30
With date/spouse	25
With children	7
With relatives	9
TOTAL	100%

Marital Status

	Percentage
Married	63%
Single	37
TOTAL	100%

How Far Do You Live from "Berry's"?

	Percentage
Less than 1 mile	18%
1–2 miles	17
3–4 miles	16

5–6 miles	15
7–8 miles	11
9–10 miles	7
11–15 miles	10
15 miles or more	6
TOTAL	100%

How Far Do You Work from "Berry's"?

	Percentage
Less than 1 mile	21%
1–2 miles	24
3–4 miles	14
5–6 miles	11
7–8 miles	2
9–10 miles	11
11–15 miles	7
15 miles or more	10
TOTAL	100%

Family Income

	Percentage
Under $17,000	33%
$17,000–$32,000	39
Over $32,000	28
TOTAL	100%

How Would You Rate Your Dining Experience?
(By Number of Fast-Food Visits in Last Two Months)

Rating	One Visit	2–4	5–8	9 or More	Total
Great	20%	13%	36%	31%	27%
Good	60	74	46	43	51
Average	0	13	9	19	15
Fair	20	0	9	5	5
Poor	0	0	0	2	2
TOTAL	100%	100%	100%	100%	100%

(N) = 1542

How Would You Rate Your Dining Experience?
(By Type of Visit)

Rating	Take-Out	Eat-In	Drive-Through	Total
Great	17%	27%	100%	27%
Good	67	51	0	51
Average	0	15	0	15
Fair	0	6	0	5
Poor	16	1	0	2
TOTAL	100%	100%	100%	100%

(N) = 1542

How Would You Rate Your Dining Experience?
(By Respondent's Age Group)

Rating	Under 18	19–24	25–34	35–49	50 or Above	Total
Great	71%	33%	14%	33%	0%	26%
Good	29	43	54	59	80	51
Average	0	14	20	8	0	14
Fair	0	5	9	0	20	6
Poor	0	5	3	0	0	3
TOTAL	100%	100%	100%	100%	100%	100%

(N) = 1542

How Would You Rate Your Dining Experience?
(By Day of Interview)

Rating	Weekday	Weekend	Total
Great	23%	30%	26%
Good	54	49	51
Average	10	17	14
Fair	10	2	6
Poor	3	2	3
TOTAL	100%	100%	100%

(N) = 1542

How Would You Rate Your Dining Experience?
(By Marital Status)

Rating	Married	Single	Total
Great	16%	45%	26%
Good	57	41	51
Average	15	10	14
Fair	10	0	6
Poor	2	4	3
TOTAL	100%	100%	100%

(N) = 1542

How Would You Rate Your Dining Experience?
(By Family Income)

Rating	Under $17,000	$17,000– $32,000	Over $32,000	Total
Great	27%	28%	10%	22%
Good	41	54	71	55
Average	23	7	14	14
Fair	5	7	5	6
Poor	4	4	0	3
TOTAL	100%	100%	100%	100%

(N) = 1542

Index